STRONGER THAN EVIL

STRONGER THAN EVIL

The Devil — Recognizing Him, Overcoming Him, and Avoiding Him

Father Gabriel Amorth
Roberto Italo Zanini

Translated by Nicholas Reitzug

SOPHIA INSTITUTE PRESS
Manchester, New Hampshire

First published in Italian as *Più Forti Del Male* by Edizioni San Paolo, Milan, Italy in 2010.

Cover by Updatefordesign Studio
Cover image: *St Anthony tormented by Demons* (Alamy EKY2WE)

Sophia Institute Press
Box 5284, Manchester, NH 03108
1-800-888-9344
www.SophiaInstitute.com

Sophia Institute Press is a registered trademark of Sophia Institute.

paperback ISBN 979-8-88911-116-0

ebook ISBN 979-8-88911-117-7

Library of Congress Control Number: 2024944137

First printing

Publisher's Note

The interview-like conversation between Fr. Amorth and journalist Roberto Italo Zanini is woven together seamlessly in the book. To aid the reader in differentiating between the two, *Fr. Amorth's words are presented in italics* and Roberto Zanini's words are given in roman type.

Contents

STRONGER THAN EVIL

Prologue

That morning, I had attended three exorcisms. They were not tender affairs. I had no doubts about the existence of the devil, but if I had still had any, they would have melted like snow in the sunlight. During the Mass that always preceded the rite of liberation, in the church near the subway station just a few steps from St. John Lateran, I had naïvely attempted to sleuth out who among those present could be the possessed ones. Fr. Amorth had told me that some in attendance were simply there to receive the blessing without having anything happen to them. Others with a long history of exorcisms behind them have a very diminished repulsion for the sacred. I must confess that I identified some strange people, so to speak. But I had to rethink everything when I discovered that I had not noticed anything peculiar in the only two people present who underwent the exorcism. Others did not attend Mass and arrived later, according to their appointments.

Of these two people, one in particular impressed me. A quite normal young lady of about twenty-five, she was sweet in her manners, very reserved. While Fr. Amorth was preparing for the exorcisms in the room next to the church, blessing all the objects and people present, including the bottled water that over the course of the hot summer morning would be needed to quench our thirst, she was waiting her turn in the church. She had certainly been praying, for I had seen her absorbed, seated on one of the last pews. Her gaze was fixed on the tabernacle. At least, this is how things appeared to me.

During the first exorcism, Fr. Amorth had invited me to sit next to him. Taking a chair, I approached the bed on one side of the room where the woman about to undergo the rite had laid down. Then, as I noticed many people around her, I found an excuse to back off a bit. There was ample space, so I took my chair to about the middle of the room, next to a table on which objects for the blessing had been placed. This was the prudent gesture of one who prefers to keep a distance from what is about to happen, but was also part of my training as a journalist who seeks the best visual perspective to keep the whole scene under control. Near me were two women with rosaries in their hands. Two people were seated on the other side of the room, a man and a woman. They too, after having rummaged in their pockets, were running through the beads of their rosaries. From that position, I could see everything. I could not believe there could be so many people.

Next to the bed there were three other priests besides Fr. Amorth. There was also a man and three women. Two people watched the door. During the exorcisms, in fact, the church was closed, and so it was necessary to open the gate for those who had later appointments.

Fr. Amorth had mentioned how attentive the exorcists were in choosing their collaborators and, in a certain way, were meticulous about the people who made up their prayer group. Because *every exorcist needs people who will pray with him, next to him. It is through prayer that the devil is forced to reveal himself and then to flee.* From his words, however, I had not understood that these were volunteers: a group of people who, twice a week, from eight in the morning, meet in this church to pray until Hell is uncovered.

Seated next to them, I too put my hand to my rosary ring, which I always wear. I wanted to pray. I felt it would be useful. I had never believed I could pray with such intensity. Marian prayer and devotion have always been a life companion to me. That day, I truly understood why we pray, and how we cannot live as free men without prayer.

Fr. Amorth began reciting the long formula of the exorcism in Latin. He always uses that one and not the new form because he considers it *too tender*, and therefore, *entirely useless*. To explain the concept to me, he used the colorful expression of a famous exorcist who died years ago, the Benedictine Dom Pellegrino Ernetti: *To banish the devil, the intercession of the Holy Spirit is needed, and then just hard punches and blows. All the rest is worthless.*

The four priests prayed out loud. A young lady, seated next to the bed, began to sing in Gregorian chant with a soft voice creating a background melody. The woman lying there was already starting to get agitated. Her contorted mouth drooled. Behind her, a robust woman was holding her head and wiping her with a handkerchief. Then the contortions moved through her body. The people around the bed held her arms and legs. Only her stomach was now moving with sudden jerks. It shook with unnatural movements that defy description and comprehension, unless one believes there was something within her pushing in all directions, as if in search of an exit. Groans came out of her mouth. Her words, at first incomprehensible, became increasingly coherent. The voice was not human, absolutely beyond compare with her voice after the exorcism. Once the prayer was over, Fr. Amorth began interrogating the woman. Not her, of course, but that something that was agitating within that, amid the various rude sounds and noises, occasionally said, as if imploringly:

"No ... no! I don't want to come out! I don't want to come out!"

He asked who it was, because many demons (as I discovered, those to be considered the leaders of their brigade) have their own name, and each has precise traits. He asked how many there were, because it often happens that not only one demon is possessing a person.

Although reluctantly, the voice gave an answer, hissing, terrible to hear, to which I gave little attention to be honest, busy as I was praying the Rosary. I do remember one thing distinctly. When Fr. Amorth asked who it was who had cursed the woman (in other words, who had invoked the devil to enter her), a terrifying, choked yell came forth:

"Sabrina ... It was Sabrina ... Damn her!"

Of course, I thought, as a chilling shudder ran through me, the devil is the accuser, the deceiver. First he exploits his slaves, then he denounces and curses them openly.

After the blessing, the woman calmed down. With difficulty, they convinced her to make the sign of the cross and recite several prayers. Then she sat up and remained seated on the edge of the bed. She seemed distressed, but not as much as one would expect. She drank and thanked him repeatedly as she approached the table to make another appointment. At that point, I saw Fr. Amorth repeat the same gestures he had made when we had to arrange the day and time for our summer chats. The same one I saw him making later with the other patients (as he calls them), exactly the same ones he makes every time someone asks him for an appointment, even the rare times he grants one over the phone. And the terms of the contract are not random, made by the half hour and quarter hour. Fr. Amorth took out the page of the calendar that he always uses as his appointment book, with the lined spaces for the days of the month all filled with scribblings, hours, references, drawings, cancellations, reconsiderations, and words superimposed:

> *Wednesday ... Might work! No, but that morning I have a person coming ... it's a peaceful case, but a bit complicated. But maybe there's not enough time. And at 11 it's*

> *too hot ... let's do it tomorrow. At 9. 9 is good. Okay, I'll write 8:30, it's cooler.*
>
> Tomorrow, in fact, I have a commitment.
>
> *So next week, then.*
>
> But isn't that too late?
>
> *In fact, it is a bit late. So, Wednesday. There's little time, but it might work.*

The woman had agreed on an appointment for three weeks later, and she went away peaceful. Before leaving the church, although it seemed inappropriate to ask for information after what I had seen and heard, but for the sake of reporting, I asked her how she had become aware of the presence of the evil one within her, how she had understood it, and what the symptoms were.

> "You're not at all aware of his presence. You don't know what you have within you. You feel you've changed and you don't know why. That you're not well and you don't know why. I have terrible stomach pain. I've had medical tests done and therapies without any results. Then you meet someone who tells you, 'But could it be that ...' Then you go to the exorcist and it all becomes clear."
>
> *And after the exorcisms, how do you feel?*
>
> "I feel well. It feels like I'm born again. I'm able to do what I used to do. Then, however, after a week, ten days, it all returns as before, and you can't wait for the day you come back here."

I would have liked to inquire about Sabrina, but only asked if there had been some reason for all this malevolence being unleashed against her. At first she said no. Then, she added something else. But her eyes were already filling with tears. She was obviously under stress, and a simple sign of comprehension for her pain was enough to help her understand that there was no need to go any further. We said goodbye, and she was on her way.

Meanwhile, the twenty-five-year-old woman had entered the room. Sympathetic, a bit shy, she was lying down on the bed. It was her third or fourth exorcism, and Fr. Amorth had told me that he had not yet succeeded in understanding anything. *At times, there can be demons that try to conceal themselves. It all points to the fact that the devil is working in a person, but nothing happens during the exorcisms. I remember one case in particular. It concerned a woman. I had been exorcising her for months and no sign of the devil came forth. I consulted with Fr. Candido, my teacher, who advised me to continue despite the lack of results. I continued. After a year and a half of exorcisms, the devil could no longer conceal himself and he burst out. He had hoped to the very end not to be discovered. He was counting on the exhaustion of the exorcist.*

The young lady was lying down now, and the four priests had begun the ritual prayer. At a certain point, her abdomen started to jerk incredibly. It was truly amazing, even compared to what I had seen earlier. Despite how thin the woman was, it was as if a basketball was bouncing around inside her. Incomprehensible words came out of her mouth — laments, disconnected sentences, and hysterical laughter that could only be described as diabolical. Fr. Amorth asked her the question indicated by the ritual and obtained only grunts and laments in response, while her belly continued its incredible rhythmic movements.

We still cannot get anything out of this woman, he exclaimed, exchanging glances with his collaborators. Thus, he concluded the exorcism with some disappointment.

I had continued running through my rosary, waiting for the young woman to regain the least bit of a smile. Then I stood up and left. I wanted to ask her some questions as well, but after having shared impressions with two women I had met during my time with Fr. Amorth, I saw her stop in the empty church where a parish priest was celebrating Mass. She approached the altar to receive Communion. Then another exorcism began, and I went to see what was happening. This time, however, I remained in the doorway. I was feeling the weight of the two preceding ones, and I felt I could take no more.

The patient was a man. He too was quite young. He was accompanied by his girlfriend. They told me he was a TV actor, among the lesser-known ones, acting in dramas and soap operas. From the moment he began having these problems, he could no longer work. A classic case of a curse. He had been coming to Fr. Amorth for many months, and said he was already feeling better. He told him, with great satisfaction, that in the following days he would be able to interview for a part. Together with the girl, he placed on the table a large paper bag from which he drew out objects to show the exorcist, which he promptly invited him to burn. Among the objects was a pillow with evident stains of dried blood, the origins of which they had no idea, and a necklace with a wooden charm of a strange form. The actor told how, the day before, a stranger had given it to him along the street.

When the exorcism began, his agitation was so intense that the people around the bed, including the priests, had to use all their strength to hold him down. He made noises, belched, and began gurgling deeply. He cursed God both in a loud voice and while mumbling. Then there was disjointed laughter, sardonic cackling, animalesque snorting, threats, and nastiness of every sort, while his expression assumed the most terrifying sneers.

I remained in the doorway and left before the exorcism concluded, following one of Fr. Amorth's collaborators who needed to smoke, out to the streetside stairs of the church to get some fresh air. Along the central thoroughfare of Rome, daily life raced by. Every now and then, an elderly person would stop in front of the gate asking to enter. With great kindness, the woman explained that it was not possible at that moment. And together we spoke of the fact that if the people only knew ... but knew what? That the devil exists? That there are those who carry Hell within them against their will and that they would gladly be liberated from it? And those who harbor that Hell within with love, or rather with hatred? And those who advertise the fact with great nonchalance? And those who welcome and spread it with superficiality, without even realizing the seriousness of their actions? These are the people who should know. But there must be someone to tell them, to explain to them what it is like, without falsifying, without feigning, without fear of not being believed. Truth for truth's sake, in the conviction that the devil, evil, takes advantage of the falsehood that we spread about him.

And then, *the devil is a type of confirmation of the existence of God*. How many times have we heard Fr. Amorth say this? And after having witnessed and prayed during those exorcisms I was even more convinced of this, because never as in those moments does one feel part of the divine project of love. A paradox of faith: Love for God, prayer to God, does not consist in placing them in contrast with diabolical malevolence. Rather, love for God acquires new validity from knowledge of the demoniacal. As the expert in martial arts takes advantage of the strength of his adversary to throw him to the ground, so too does the prayer of the man of faith draw from evil the renewed stimulus to hasten its defeat. Sure, to entrust one's life to the highest good one does not need to experience the abyss of evil. Probably not. *But life is a continual battle with evil, and in order to fight one must know. To vanquish one's enemy whose main weapon is deception, full knowledge is halfway to salvation. Love which is obtained through prayer is the triumph.*

What I felt within me at that moment, I know I saw and recognized. I saw it and recognized it so well that I was left profoundly amazed. I wonder how my two friends and the priests and volunteers who prayed during the exorcisms were able to stay calm after having witnessed the same things. In fact, they kept telling me that, in the end, these were "only a few of the simplest cases. There's nothing to fear, because faith, prayer, and the love of God conquer everything."

I too was convinced of the fact that good is stronger than evil, thanks to the crutch of my poor faith that continued to sustain me, but I had had enough that morning. I would have waited until the end of the last exorcism, I would have greeted Fr. Amorth and returned to the business of the day ahead of me, knowing that nothing would ever be the same again.

A little breath of calm that lasted the space of that brief and intense chat on the steps outside the church. At that moment, someone left the church looking for me: "Fr. Amorth told me to look for you because this is a particular case and he wants you to see it."

I had just picked out the step I was going to sit down on, but I was too late. I thought, "I'll sit down and watch the people along the street and pray for them." I had already gotten out my rosary. The only right thing I had done. It was my weapon and, strengthened by it, I went back in.

Lying on the bed was a woman, quite robust. On the couch next to the chair I had been using there was an older woman, the mother, and on her knees a child of seven or eight, her child. I sat down, and then a doubt came to mind, very naïve, but I discovered just how naïve only afterward. I turned to one of my friends and asked,

"Should this child really be staying here? Wouldn't it be better to have him leave?"

"Let him stay," she replied, accompanying her words with a reassuring gesture.

I sat down again without understanding. The grandmother, with her grandson, was sitting next to me. The exorcism began, and this time there was no need for the prayer to continue long to see its first effects. The woman began to agitate, and so did the child. The more the woman agitated, the more the child did too. The woman let out a scream, she ranted and raved, and the child wheezed, emitting strange sounds. I looked at him for an instant and realized only then that he had an intellectual disability. The woman screamed more and more, foaming at the mouth, and the people around the bed were hard pressed to keep her down. The devil had already expressed his desire not to leave her, amid disjointed sneers. Every so often, one heard clearly his cry: "Help! Help!"

These requests were at times shouted, at times gnashed and hissed. It was the devil asking for the help of his peers, they later told me. It happens when there is more than one demon possessing the person and some of them understand they are about to be expelled. This sign instructed Fr. Amorth that it was time to begin his interrogation precisely with this topic:

> *How many of you are there?*
>
> Many.
>
> *How many?*
>
> Twenty-five.

This answer satisfied the exorcist, because the previous time the number was much higher. The interrogation continued. The woman's agitation reached its climax, and the voice became truly terrifying when the questions were directed to her son:

> *What does your child have?*
>
> You have not understood.... You have not understood! He is bound to me.... To me!
>
> *What curse is he under?*

At first there was no response to this, but only noises even louder than the previous ones. The child in his grandmother's arms had now become unrestrainable. Fr. Amorth insisted. This time he was no longer asking, but commanding.

What curse is he under?

Diabolical ... A diabolical curse!

I had never experienced such an intensity of malice in so few words: impossible to forget. Maybe Fr. Amorth was right. I had to be present at that exorcism to have a clear idea of the gospel truth he had told me about: the liberation from demons, the healing of the sick, the remission of sins — all go together. They are different sides of the same coin.

When she left the room and had reached the church door, I tried to speak with the woman. She wanted to go, to live those few moments of peace that the exorcism had given her. She too, in fact, would continue to have the same problems. I asked her how it is to live with such a presence.

"Bad," she replied, "very bad. At times it gets unbearable. But what really hurts is that everyone has always considered me to be crazy."

Mental Illness or an Affliction of the Soul?

Once, my friend Fr. Fausto Negrini asked the devil during an exorcism, "By now, you possess few people. No one even knows you exist anymore." The devil responded, "It's enough to go to the insane asylums to see how many people I possess."

Satan is defeated, expelled, cast out, but he is able to drag many people along with him. The problem of presumed psychiatric illnesses is, in this sense, a very serious one. Psychiatrists do not realize this. While medicines for the body have made giant leaps forward, with great progress in the understanding and the cure of illnesses, as far as concerns the knowledge of the psyche, of the causes and the therapies of psychic illnesses, still lags far behind. It can be said that in most cases, psychiatrists are shooting blanks. There are some among them who swear that more or less 70 percent of the work of a psychiatrist has to do with remedying the erroneous therapies of another psychiatrist. I have often collaborated with psychiatrists, although it is difficult to find believers among them, because most idolize Freud. Quite often, their findings are fundamental. There are many cases, however, in which the sickness seems psychiatric, but then turns out not to be; in others, the psychiatric illness is heavily aggravated by the demonic affliction.

In his *Guide to the Summa Theologica*, Walter Farrell makes an interesting observation in which he associates the diabolical inspiration of Nietzsche's work with "those disturbances of the intellect that, over the following years would plunge the philosopher into the immense abyss of madness." The thought that there might be a causal relationship here comes to mind, though not of necessity.

I have often discussed these themes with a psychiatrist friend who has also come to many of my exorcisms and has realized what the demonic effects can be on the human psyche. At first, he did not want to believe in the devil, but then he had to admit it. He allowed me to hold a meeting with sixty high-level psychiatrists, with whom I had a most interesting discussion and about which a book was published. They asked me the most difficult questions I have ever had to face, but I was able to respond to all of them. I developed my arguments, I offered my examples, the experience of decades of work in this field, and they were incapable of giving convincing objections. In a certain sense, we defined the two areas of interest with ample precision.

At any rate, in the Gospel the two aspects are often placed together. Jesus healed the sick and cast out demons. Fr. Candido was extraordinary in this regard. He had some exceptional charisms. Often he would amaze doctors, even entire hospitals. He never got the diagnosis wrong, and sent those with psychiatric illnesses to the psychiatrists he trusted. In other cases, he performed exorcisms or prayers of healing.

For an exorcist, it is fundamental, as well as a point of extreme difficulty, to know how to distinguish an evil curse from a psychic illness. The symptoms that psychiatrists use to formulate their diagnoses are completely different from those that are of interest to exorcists. Each one must know how to stay in his own field to be mutually useful.

To clarify this point, an exorcist is very attentive to a person's sensibility to holy water. A case that occurred to Fr. Candido is suggestive. He was performing an exorcism, but when he discovered he had no holy water he sent an assistant to fetch some. As soon as the man returned with the tub and aspergillum, the devil whom Fr. Candido was interrogating said through the person being exorcised, "You can wash your snout with that water." It was only simple water because the tub had been filled from the faucet in the sacristy. The devil understood the difference immediately.

Quite often, just a splash of holy water is enough to cause the demon inside a person to start shouting: "Stop, stop, it's burning me!" Precisely this reluctance of the devil makes the test between holy water and simple water fundamental in some cases. At times I ask relatives to do the test to see if the person they suspect to be possessed really has a demonic problem. Not so long ago, a case such as this happened to a twenty-year-old girl. From what the mother told me, she was strongly suspected to be under demonic possession. So I advised her secretly to prepare, using holy water, a dish the girl would like and to serve it to the entire family. The woman decided to make a soup. No one knew about the experiment. They all ate it except the girl, who set it aside, making up the excuse, "I don't feel like eating this soup." The next day, the woman carried out the test again, placing the holy water in another recipe, with the same result.

Aversion to the sacred is another important sign. I remember a young man who threw out or destroyed all the sacred images he found. If a priest came to the house for the Easter blessing or for some other reason, without attracting attention, he would close himself into his bedroom. I counselled his father to recite in his heart a prayer in the boy's presence, choosing a normal moment of family life. The father began reciting silently the Our Father at the dinner table, and his son suddenly and violently stood up and ordered him to stop.

Given the great number of cases and the many people who have real need of assistance, although exorcisms are not needed in every case, before making an appointment, I am very selective and I demand a lot of information. The first thing I require is a medical diagnosis of the disturbances they are suffering. I then ask if the person has a regular prayer life. I ask when the disturbance began, and if the first manifestation occurred in concomitance with a particular event. I ask how the disturbance manifests itself, if it rages with shouts, noises, spasms, and abnormal movements. I ask what the person's reaction is to blessings. In many cases, I send questionnaires with a series of questions. When reading the responses, if I do not find suspicious symptoms, I avoid receiving the person in order to dedicate myself to other cases because, like I said, there are always so many requests. Almost every day I find the answering machine full and unable to record any more messages.

At any rate, an exorcism is the last thing that must be performed, and only when all other remedies have failed to produce an effect. For many people, it is enough for them to feel spiritually accepted and guided, to have their needs listened to, to pray with them, to teach them to pray even for the person causing their problems, guiding them in preparing a good confession. Then there are also many people with fixations, paranoias, under the delusion of being possessed, pursued by the devil, and so forth.

An infallible method is also the common liturgy for healing and liberation. If they have neither negative reactions nor specific symptoms in these cases, they can be sure not to have them during an exorcism either. Discernment is of course needed regarding what happens during the Masses for healing and liberation as well. It can happen that someone starts yelling desperately or is thrown to the ground or becomes violent. Quite often, however, these are problems of hysteria or suggestion. At other times, we already know the people we need to keep an eye on because they have been reported to us. Something like this, for example, happened to me with Milingo, when he celebrated healing and liberation Masses every first Monday of the month. There were enormous crowds. And there were many cases of hysteria and suggestion. Before the celebration, Milingo warned me of the presence of a possessed man who would have certain symptoms, which then came to pass.

Milingo? I happened to meet him and to hear about him from people who frequented him, and to participate in his celebrations. At the end of it all, I had the sensation one has when one loses a beautiful opportunity. Was he an exorcist who allowed himself to be bound by the devil?

His is a very sad story. We are friends. He occasionally calls me. He comes to visit me. We talk. I pray for him every day. I ask the Holy Spirit to give him the grace of humility. Humility is fundamental. Without humility there can be no contrition — one cannot recognize one's errors or have the courage to turn around. Undoubtedly, he has been treated unfairly, but he went too far in his protest and dissent from the Church. For her part, the Church did much to welcome him back with open arms. He really needs to be drenched in humility. Then, erroneous knowledge, the wrong influences, the Reverend Sun Myung Moon, that woman who keeps a tight rein on him, and the unfathomable Mysteries of the human soul. Judas as well expelled demons, like all the other apostles, but then Satan entered him. The power to cast out demons is one thing; one's choices and personal life are another.

Either Jesus or the Devil

"Where the fear of God guards the entrance, there the enemy cannot find a way in." The phrase is taken from the *Words of Admonition* of St. Francis, and it illustrates perfectly how a life of prayer and sacraments, lived in the grace of God, protects us from evil spells, from temptations, and from every type of diabolical influence.

Rosa, or Signora Rosa as everyone calls her, explains and demonstrates it very well through her life. She is an authentic point of reference for those who turn to Fr. Amorth, for whom she is the living historical memory, his most faithful collaborator. She and her family, her husband and six male children, were tormented by evil curses for thirty-two years until she happened to meet Fr. Candido Amantini, Fr. Amorth's mentor. He was a member of the Passionist Fathers who died in 1992, very well known in Rome as the exorcist of the Scala Santa. From that moment, Rosa states, "the grace of God entered our lives. Everything changed radically."

Theirs was a long and difficult struggle. "Sicknesses came one after another. We were all sick. Terrible, debilitating illnesses, some afflicting my children from birth. The doctors did not know what to do. My children underwent numerous surgeries, because the tests and medical examinations always turned up the presence of serious diseases, but the surgical procedures often failed to find anything. Cut open and sewn up again, and all for nothing. The affliction continued. When our youngest son was seriously ill at the Bambin Gesù Hospital of the Holy See, a doctor listened to our story and recommended we consult Fr. Candido. After many years of suffering, our rebirth had begun, and we understood what had happened to us."

It all began in the month of December, more or less two months before Rosa's wedding. "My husband had had an argument with his mother. He cannot stand laziness and had criticized his brother, who always had an excuse for not working. He insisted it was not true that he was ill, but that he simply didn't want to work. My mother-in-law lost her patience. 'That's not true,' she replied, 'you're a liar and you'll find out what it means not to feel well!' It might seem strange, but a few days later, my husband's legs stiffened up. Our wedding date had been set for February. We were married, although he could hardly stand up straight. From that moment we were plunged into an abyss of endless suffering. It's not easy to understand such things. A lot of people don't believe it. It's so hard to find doctors who understand you. They think you've gone mad. You end up on the verge of desperation.

"One of my mother-in-law's curses, the last one to have an effect, struck after we had met Fr. Candido. She said to my husband, 'May you get cancer of the tongue!' After just a few hours he was already starting to feel ill. The tests and diagnoses of the doctors were implacable: cancer of the throat and of the root of the tongue. When Fr. Candido found out about this he invited us to meet with him. We met one Sunday after the Mass. He called us aside. He exorcised my husband's throat. The healing was immediate and complete. Later investigation certified that there was no longer anything there."

From this experience, a united, strengthened family emerged with a strong faith. Rosa dedicated herself entirely to helping people who suffer from the same problems she had suffered. It was Fr. Candido who asked her to follow Fr. Amorth and to give him a hand.

"I did it out of gratitude and obedience, and since that day I have been in his service. I have helped many people with serious diabolical problems who did not know where to turn, who to trust."

Rosa speaks with a zeal, a simplicity, and a faith that are not easy to find in others. It is clear from her words and from the tears she occasionally struggles to suppress that those experiences pushed her to the limit. But she is proud of this. This is her life now, and she would never turn back, despite her age and the many infirmities inherited from her difficult existence.

"When you have suffered that much and received the greatest graces, you can only desire that others who suffer might enjoy the same goodness you have." These were the words, not of Rosa, but of the friend who was seated next to her throughout our conversation who accompanies her in her mission. For some time now she has been suffering from Parkinson's, as Fr. Candido had foreseen.

"But when you deal with these matters," the journalist in me asked, with hesitation, "are you not afraid of exposing yourself to something too big, something uncontrollable?"

The first to respond was Rosa's friend. "I too, at first, was afraid. How can you not be in the face of such manifestations? Then I understood that if you lead a life of prayer, sacraments, and surrender to the Lord and to the Virgin Mary, you have nothing to fear. This is true for you and for all those near to you. A united family in which faith is lived and visible, where there is prayer, is under great protection. Good is stronger than evil."

The two women looked at me. They understood my difficulty. They invited me to have faith, to pray, to go forward with this complicated task. Not convinced, I insisted, "It is not easy to put together all the stories I have heard and seen with my own eyes. They are so enormous. And I have to tell them in a way that people will not reject them, that they do not think they are just clever scenes from a horror film or beliefs from another, primitive epoch, beliefs that have no right to be held in the third millennium." This time it was Rosa who answered first, "Pray to the Holy Spirit and you'll find that your problems will vanish."

Not to Fly without Wings

Do not fear, because *good is infinitely stronger than evil.* Fr. Amorth halted a moment, lost in thought, a memory whose wave he then rode passionately: *Who knows how many curses have been hurled at me? How many temptations! Even Fr. Candido, from the very beginning of our collaboration, had reassured me: "Fear not, the Lord is protecting us."*

Sometime before that, when the Cardinal Vicar of Rome at the time, Ugo Poletti, had assigned to me the role of exorcist, I entrusted myself entirely to the protection and the help of the Virgin Mary. Wrap me in your mantel, I asked of her in prayer, and with you I shall be safe. I have felt and lived this protection over the years as something inviolable. I have this certainty when I pray, when I recite the Rosary, when I visit Marian sanctuaries. I have had proof of this from various demons, from the mouths of people whom I have exorcised: "We can do nothing to you because you are too well protected."

And to think that I had no intention of being an exorcist. Cardinal Poletti took me by surprise, in such a way that I could not refuse.

It was a delight to hear from Fr. Gabriele the story of how Poletti pinned him into being an exorcist. The memory made his eyes brighten with joy, as when telling jokes, especially the ones he heard from the mouth of Padre Pio: *a character who, when he was in the mood and had some free time, was so fun.*

In Rome at that time, I often ran into the cardinal. We were friends and he really appreciated my jokes. When I had new ones, I went to visit him. That afternoon, I rang the doorbell of his apartment and he came to open the door in person. As always, after my anecdotes, we talked about the things one talks about, and about pastoral problems. Eventually the conversation came around to Fr. Candido, whom everyone considered a saintly man, but who was overloaded with work. The cardinal paused to consider the great number of people who sought Fr. Candido for the Mass or exorcisms. The Holy Stairs were just a few minutes away from the cardinal's apartment. Spontaneously, I mentioned that I knew about those things because I know Fr. Candido well.

Hearing this, the cardinal gazed at me with a smile, and said, "Ill as he is, and with all the people who ask for him, he's in great need of help."

While he expressed with visible compassion these sentiments of comprehension for the work of the exorcist, he was looking on his desk and in its drawers for letterhead paper. When he found a sheet, he was silent and began to write. I watched him as he wrote. Then he raised his eyes after having signed his name, handed me the letter, and said, "Good, this is your new assignment."

"My new assignment?" I said, emphasizing my amazement. I then began to read the letter. It was my nomination as exorcist of the Diocese of Rome, assigned to Fr. Candido as his assistant and apprentice. Naturally, I attempted to protest: "Your Eminence, you know I am not capable. I cannot. You know I'm not suited. I like to tell jokes, to get into mischief."

He would have none of it. The cardinal remained implacable in his decision, convinced I would be up to the task. With a blessing and a slap on the back he accompanied me to the door, assuring me of his prayers. That afternoon I had some free time, and I went to my friend Poletti to tell one of my jokes. Now I was leaving with the assignment of exorcist. The following day, I went to Fr. Candido with that letter. I think I haven't had any free time since.

Among those who have had a certain type of spiritual life in Rome, the person of Fr. Candido is very well known. There are many who have benefitted from his work and remember him as a saint. At times, it's enough to ask at Sunday Mass to find people indebted to him.

A dear friend, now happily married with children, who as a child suffered an oppressive diabolical influence due to friendship with a musician with ties to an esoteric, occult sect, narrates his experience with the lucidity typical only of those who have had direct knowledge of the evil one and have succeeded in liberating themselves through a life of faith. "Without even realizing it, I was walking the paths of evil. I had chosen evil in my life." It was a period that he remembers as extremely sad, marked by great interior tension, by a dark desire to die. Then, his family grew concerned, and those close to him began to pressure him.

His life took off again when he participated in a Mass of healing and liberation. "There, I experienced the extraordinary effect of the peace of Jesus that surrounds you, that enters your heart. A light as of the rising sun." He began to attend meetings with Fr. Candido and Fr. Amorth, who at that time were already working together. The memory of the prayers of exorcism, of the counsel of the two priests, and of the crowded six o'clock Masses each morning at the Holy Stairs were unforgettable.

"There were so many of us, each with a heavy burden to carry. When Fr. Candido began the prayer of exorcism in Latin, it seemed the gates of Hell were thrust wide open. I remember one young lady. She was next to me. While waiting, we talked at length. She seemed completely normal. At a certain point, she started to contort and wheeze and hiss. She began speaking in ancient Greek, shouting. Others near her started to agitate as well, making noises and blaspheming.... Then I felt within me a great peace. Every time it was like that. It was like the experience of Elijah, who awaited God in the cave and after noises and tempests hears his arrival in a gentle breeze. There was silence all around me. The young lady fell to the ground in a heap. From within her I could hear a voice that was now different from that which had spoken up to that moment. A horrible groan and, quite distinct, the words in Italian: "You have found me."

The teachings of Fr. Candido continue to guide this friend and his family on the path of Christ's peace. "He told me I had to pray and from that day on I don't think I have ever stopped. Prayer must be part of your life, he told me. You must always entrust yourself to the Virgin Mary. And remember that the devil must always be rejected. Any situation that makes you feel his presence, distance yourself from it. Always preserve the freedom of your soul. In the moment you feel your interior freedom has been taken from you, distance yourself from that situation, pray more insistently. Remember that the devil is strong only with the weak and must be treated with a healthy disdain."

The many icons of Our Lady of Mercy found in so many sanctuaries come to mind. It is easy to think of the one in Monte Berico in Vicenza, for example. Mother Mary wraps in her mantel the faithful who entrust themselves to her. In some images, entire cities are placed under her mantel. There are *ex-votos* in which Mary extends her mantel over tempest-tossed ships, imploring people, the sick illuminated by divine grace. One who seeks grace but does not have recourse to her, recalls Dante, "wants his desire to fly without wings." *The Lord has given us many graces to conquer the devil. Prayer has enormous power. It is the triumph of good. And then a life of sacraments. Entrusting oneself to the protection of the Virgin Mary. Unconditional trust in Divine Mercy.*

Unfortunately, we are so often distracted. Individuals, entire communities, priests. We doze off like the apostles in the Garden of Gethsemane. Or worse, we are convinced that we can fly without wings. In that moment we must be very careful not to put our trust in the corrupt and crippled wings of the devil in our naïveté or malice. This temptation always crouches in ambush and often consists of superstitions. Even little ones, seemingly insignificant, are like open doors to the devil. Here, once more, we do well to reflect upon the story of the friend we just encountered, a story supported by numerous other witnesses.

"One day I was next to Fr. Candido. We were speaking. It was one of the usual morning meetings at St. John's and there were a lot of people, many suffering from various problems. At one point, a tiny old lady made her way through the crowd. She approached and asked, more or less like everyone else, 'Fr. Candido, you have to do me a favor.' He looked at her with the usual welcoming expression, ready to grant her request. The little old lady looked for something in her pockets and, holding it tight in both hands as one does with something precious which absolutely must not be lost, asked again, 'You must bless this crucifix for me.' Saying this, she opened her hands to show a thin necklace with a little golden cross.

"Fr. Candido seemed about to bless it when he suddenly went rigid. At that moment I realized that in the woman's hands, partly hidden by the cross, the form of a horn poked out. It was also made of gold and hung from the necklace. The priest's face grew dark and tense. His voice grew severe and resounded in the church with an authority that none of us had ever heard: 'You do not realize what you are doing. You cannot confuse Christ with these things. Go! Throw all this away! And come back only after you have chosen between Jesus and the devil.'"

The Works of the Devil

The problem of evil concerns all peoples and all ages. We know that the problem depends on the devil. This knowledge comes to us from revelation. It is the devil that generates evil and his work can be ordinary or extraordinary.

His ordinary work is normally performed through temptations. Tempting man is the activity the devil mostly dedicates himself to, and it is that which he most relishes, because through it he is able to bring about the loss of souls.

His extraordinary work is performed much more rarely through so-called evil spells.

These are delicate and complicated topics. Before confronting them, we do well to reaffirm (we shall return to this later as well) the Christian principle stated in the book of Revelation, according to which in the battle against evil it is good that triumphs; in this battle man is never alone. He can choose to be alone, but in the moment he seeks it, divine grace is ready to accompany him and provide him with the instruments necessary to fight and to win. And if we do not fall into error and persist in that error, we must know that Jesus awaits us to the very end. He wants our salvation, and his mercy is always ready to welcome us as long as we want it. No one knows better than Jesus Christ that on the path of evil it's enough to slide, whereas the path of good is always uphill. It all depends on what we choose, and the Holy Spirit is ready to fortify us.

To carry out his design, the devil uses all his means to tempt man. In this sense, modernity has offered him further assistance and people are increasingly incapable of recognizing evil. As St. John emphasizes in his First Letter, the whole world lies under the power of the evil one. The main task of the devil is to make sure man thinks exclusively about terrestrial matters. It is interesting, for example, how society, marketing, and the media convey with insistence a way of understanding beauty and bodily health as if it were the true goal in life. The great deception of being eternally beautiful, eternally healthy. Notice that the kingdom of Satan is the kingdom of deception, opposed to the Kingdom of God, which is the kingdom of truth. And only the truth will make us free (John 8:32).

In the Kingdom of God, everything that is of this world exists in function of its final end. "My kingdom," emphasized Jesus, "is not of this world." The Beatitudes are in function of the Kingdom of Heaven. Jesus never promised earthly happiness. The path that leads to Paradise always passes through Calvary. The Kingdom of God is Paradise. The goal of life is to merit it. And if one saves his soul, whatever one's fate was on this earth, that life was a success. For what will it profit a man, if he gains the whole world and forfeits his life (Matt. 16:26)? The parable of the rich man is an essential image for indicating the path of respect for the Ten Commandments.

Quite another thing is what I term, according to the classification of the Church, the extraordinary work of the devil. The concept of extraordinary *is relative to the fact that these are infrequent manifestations performed by the power of the devil, though they are not his preferred activity.*

There are four extraordinary evils provoked by the devil: possession, vexation, obsession, and infestation. Among these evils, possession is certainly the rarest phenomenon, together with infestation. Possession is the phenomenon in which the devil takes possession of the body of a person against his will and therefore without in fact influencing directly the person's soul. There have been saints who have been possessed by the devil. To be clear, if one who is possessed were to die, it would not have any influence over his salvation. In possession, the devil can use the body of the possessed person at will and therefore the actions carried out by the possessed are not conscious actions. St. Mary of Jesus Crucified, the only Arabian saint, born near Nazareth, blasphemed and did unspeakable things when she was possessed by the devil.

During exorcisms, one often witnesses extraordinary phenomena unleashed by the devil. Movements and contortions of parts of the body that would be simply inconceivable in a normal person, bodily levitation, sudden changes of one's voice, people who barely speak their own language speaking in the most random of languages. Beware, however. The seriousness of the situation is not always directly proportional to the unsightliness of what appears. It is not the extraordinary nature of the manifestations that indicates whether we are in the presence of difficult cases, situations in which liberation is difficult to obtain.

Just as there are cases in which the devil stays hidden and it might take years for the person to be liberated, so there are other cases in which, despite striking diabolical manifestations, the person is liberated quickly. At times it is difficult to obtain complete liberation. On this matter, I must say that Fr. Candido disabused me from the very start of every illusion, inviting me to exercise humility. Putting the brake on my initial enthusiasm, he said: "Don't expect to see someone liberated at the end of an exorcism. It is a very rare event."

In fact, I have never had the pleasure of seeing a person completely liberated after an exorcism. Liberation comes about almost always in other circumstances. Usually in sacred contexts, especially in sanctuaries. Fr. Candido, for example, was particularly devoted to Lourdes and Loreto, where he often sent people he exorcised because he happened to notice that many of them were liberated there. In Loreto we have had many cases of liberation. But it can happen anywhere, entering a church, even during a simple prayer or while carrying out one's daily tasks.

A great school of humility. The people, these great sufferers, come to us with expectations. They have an extreme need of help. They often knock at many doors without finding a response to their needs. They go to hospitals, doctors, psychiatrists, psychiatric wards, they have taken medicine, spent great sums of money on psychoanalysis, undergone surgical operations, at times repeatedly, at times to no effect. They have spoken with their parish priests, knocking on many doors, but they have not found anyone who would listen to them in the depths and comprehend their terrible drama. There are too few exorcists, and many priests, even bishops and theologians, underestimate the problem, running from it as if it were superstition. Thus, these people, after having found walls of incomprehension and ignorance, when they come to us they surrender themselves completely. But we are only useless servants, good for nothings. We are simple instruments in the hands of God. We are not the ones who liberate from the devil, but Jesus Christ. We, on behalf of the Church, act in the name of Jesus Christ, whose exorcisms narrated in the Gospel, as the Catechism of the Catholic Church *(para. 550) recalls, "anticipate Jesus' great victory over the 'Ruler of this world' (John 12:31)."*

A truth of faith repeated explicitly by John Paul II on August 20, 1986, speaking to exorcists: "The Church participates in the victory of Christ over the devil: Christ, in fact, gave his disciples the power to cast out demons. The Church exercises this victorious power through faith in Christ and prayer which, in specific cases, can assume the form of an exorcism."

Returning to the singularity of diabolical manifestations, one of the simplest and most rapid that has ever occurred to me presented itself as very complicated. One day my friend the Franciscan friar came to me. A robust fellow, who with two others was holding tightly a very agitated young man. He was a simple farmer who had grown up in the countryside, had very poor education, and had never left his hometown. During the exorcism, he was agitated and spoke continuously in perfect English. I even needed an interpreter to understand. "I am Lucifer, king of scorpions," he said.

It really seemed a terrible case. There were even moments of levitation. One day, during the interview we usually do with the devil during the exorcism, I asked him, "When are you going to leave?" The answer from that moment on was always the same: "On June 21, at eleven o'clock."

I exorcised him twice a week. At that time, I was working in Via Merulana, in the monastery of the friars of the Church of St. Anthony. The first time was in February, and I have to say, I never had such a fast case. By around June 21, to verify the matter, I made an appointment for the following day. The young man came to me calm, peaceful as I had never seen him. I had him tell me what happened. "I was in the fields working," he said. "Suddenly, I think I let out a great yell. I looked around afraid. Then I felt better. Now I'm well."

Then I performed the exorcism, but nothing happened. I had him come another time and repeated the rite of exorcism. Nothing. He was liberated. And he was no longer able to say a word in English. He had never studied English and could not speak it.

This case serves also to explain why it is necessary to ask the devil when he intends to leave, how much time he has been granted. The ritual foresees this explicitly. When possible, one should ask even the day and the hour. The devil knows perfectly well he has little time at his disposal. At any rate, one reads in the twelfth chapter of the book of Revelation, clarifying in part what we have said and will consider later: "Now the salvation and the power and the kingdom of our God and the authority of his Christ have come, for the accuser of our brethren has been thrown down, who accuses them day and night before our God. And they have conquered him by the blood of the Lamb and by the word of their testimony, for they loved not their lives even unto death. Rejoice then, O Heaven and you that dwell therein! But woe to you, O earth and sea, for the devil has come down to you in great wrath, because he knows that his time is short!" (Rev. 12:10–12).

For this reason, he hastens in his attempt to bring as many people as possible to damnation. Naturally, one must always verify with cross references what the devil says during the exorcism because quite often he is a liar.

I remember a girl who was disturbed from the time she was sixteen. During the exorcism I asked, "When did you enter her?" "At sixteen," he answered.

After the exorcism, I had a long interview with the girl, and separately with her parents to know precisely when the first symptoms had begun. I had confirmation that in fact the first maleficent influences were manifested at sixteen.

Quite different is the problem of vexation. Vexations are enormous evils invoked on men without the presence of possession. The case of Rosa's family we learned about is a perfect example. The vexed person is not possessed by the devil. The pain, sickness, and evils they suffer are so great as to limit their freedom. Naturally, this can happen in various ways. One can be vexed physically: a sickness, strong pain, a number of sicknesses at the same time; or mentally: quite common is the case of exhaustion, depression; or affectively: one is incapable of falling in love; or even professionally: economic enterprises that fail suddenly, unmotivated firing, inability to find work.

The problems of vexation are manifold and are almost always generated by curses. Among the most common cases is that of a flourishing economic activity that, because of a curse, starts to decline inexplicably. One could say that it was due to the inability of the entrepreneur or a change in the market. When it is a matter, as has happened to me, of a shop that was well launched, placed in a great location for commercial activity, but from one day to the next loses all of its clients, perhaps to the advantage of the competition that just opened up, it is difficult to think of entrepreneurial incompetence or of the lack of appeal of the merchandise. This is true above all if the merchandise and the prices are the same as the competition and the businessman had always been esteemed by his clients.

When someone suffers this economic downturn and comes to us to ask for help, it often happens that the true motives emerge almost immediately. We go to the store, give the blessing periodically, at times Mass is celebrated there, prayers of liberation are made, and one notices a slow turnaround in the economic activity. It takes time, it takes faith, it takes prayer for things to return to how they were before. There are episodes, however, in which the obstinacy of the curse is so great that it is preferable to change business, because the damage done while waiting would be economically unsustainable.

Also common are cases tied to an emotional situation. A young man, after several years of dating a girl, realizes that she was not the right person for him. He breaks off the relationship in the normal manner, trying to hurt her as little as possible. The girl's mother will have none of it, and turns to a magician or a witch and thus begins a terrible agony for that young man: he cannot find work that lasts more than a few days, he is incapable of establishing another relationship, he falls ill, he can do nothing that requires the least effort. Fr. Candido healed many afflictions of this sort. The organs most often struck are the stomach and the head, both being organs required in the vital functions of eating and the affections. In the case of neuroses, nervous breakdown, and depression, as has already been said, many times it is difficult to understand what the actual causes are.

Within the category of psychic disturbances and instabilities, the phenomenon of obsession often appears. This is a diabolical evil that provokes thoughts that are frequent, obsessive, and apparently invincible, such that they lead to desperation and at times even to suicide or homicide. Since the devil can also influence our dreams, one sees how obsession can prevent one even from sleeping.

There are also phenomena regarding interventions in dreams that are much lighter, that are closely related to temptations, such as dreams tied to sexuality or to abusing one's neighbor. But there are also dreams that cause terror, that frighten and prevent one from sleeping. Mass media often exploit these topics, and we must not presume that the devil does not work through the means of modern communication. Films that provoke fear and terror; films constructed around violence, often as an end in itself; films about sex and physical or psychological abuse, especially if these are carried out with recourse to exoteric or occult practices, and even some cartoons: all of these are preferred themes in the dreams induced by the devil.

The phenomenon of infestation concerns cases, objects, and at times sacred images, or animals. These are very complicated issues; these too are often connected to curses from which it is not easy to find liberation without drastic solutions such as the dispossession of those objects.

Participating in the Redemption of the World

In light of this situation, it is essential to understand how one falls into these traps, how one becomes the victim of these diabolical actions and how to defend oneself from them. *The causes, according to the categories I have adopted and which have been accepted by the Church, are four. Two are "culpable" and two are "not culpable." It is essential, in particular, to know the "culpable" causes to be able to avoid them.*

The "not culpable" or innocent cases are quite rare because they concern a small number of great saints, ascetics, and mystics in whom God Himself allows the devil to test their souls with temptations and oppressions in order to reinforce their faith and make them undergo the devil's tactics, like Job, to know how to resist him. "Not culpable" are those who suffer evil spells and because of them are oppressed or are even possessed by the devil.

The "culpable" cases, on the other hand, involve entrusting oneself to magicians, witches, and to any form of divination. One is guilty of voluntarily abandoning the path of Christ, leading a dissolute life of sin, and abiding in fascination to the point of approaching pseudo-religious or satanic cults.

In every case, prayer is always the most excellent weapon. "Watch and pray that you may not enter into temptation," Jesus warned the apostles in the Garden of Gethsemane. An invitation that has been continually repeated in all the Marian apparitions. The prayer that Jesus taught us, the Our Father, after reciting the praises of God, the acceptance of the kingdom, the invocation for one's daily sustenance, the remission of sins, and reconciliation with one's neighbor, expressly asks God's help in temptations and aid in confronting the evil one. In fact, without God's help, we are defenseless.

At the healing of the demon-possessed man at the foot of Mt. Tabor, which we shall consider later, Jesus firmly emphasizes that without prayer, this type of divine intervention cannot be attained. *To be liberated from evil, we must pray for ourselves and for others. Many times, it is only by means of prayer that we can help people who are lost in sin and refuse every form of help. It was the father of the possessed man who prayed with insistence to Jesus that He might liberate him from that terrible influence. Many parents experience this type of pain for their children who are lost due to infatuations, the wrong friends, or reprehensible behavior. Their prayer consists in suffering, tears, and trust as well.*

In this case, it is helpful to remember the example of St. Monica, the mother of Augustine of Hippo. During her son's youth, lost in frolicking and a dissolute life as he recounts in his *Confessions*, she was always by his side, above all praying intensely to obtain from God the gift of his conversion. This trust in and fidelity to God her son would never forget, which transformed into the solid foundation of his own sanctity.

We spoke about the causes that introduce the devil into our lives and place us in his hands. The two which we defined as "not culpable" are to be considered quite rare: those in which God Himself consents to allow the devil to act, and those produced by curses.

The first can be difficult to understand in salvific logic, but it is closely tied to the lives of many saints and, before that, to the lives of many biblical figures. To understand this, one must read through Jesus' earthly mission and experience of the Cross. In essence, God allows the devil to act, knowing that the affected person, in his efforts to resist evil, is sanctified. St. John Chrysostom held, paradoxically, that "the devil is a sanctifier of souls." Furthermore, there are many examples of saints oppressed by the devil. From St. Francis to Padre Pio, the Curé d'Ars, and so forth. In this matter, the saint of Pietrelcina explained that "suffering is precious" because it makes us participants in the redemptive work of Jesus. And in the specific cases of the saints, it is Jesus Himself who asks these people to participate through their suffering in his redemptive work, and at times they offer themselves directly.

A mutual request that is formulated explicitly in visions and mystical dialogues and which, at times, is addressed to the salvation of specific people. In the Old Testament, there are many examples of this sort. The book of Tobit and the book of Job are very interesting in this regard. The work of the devil in those books is not only as the tempter but is placed in relation to the saving and liberating work of God, carried out through men. God sends His angel to Tobit and Tobias, but it is the action of the two men that renders the angel's task possible, including the liberation from the evil demon through the actions of Tobias, of his promised wife Sarah. It is the faithfulness of Job, against all odds, against all abuse carried out by evil, which sanctifies him and justifies him in the sight of God and man. Here, the devil puts God to the test through Job, and God chooses Job as the architect of the devil's defeat, as is evident in the dialogue between God and Satan in the first chapter (vv. 10–11): "Thou hast blessed the work of his hands, and his possessions have increased in the land. But put forth thy hand now, and touch all that he has, and he will curse thee to thy face." The same dialogue is repeated in the second chapter when Satan realizes that Job's faithfulness will persevere despite his economic ruin. He insists, "But put forth thy hand now, and touch his bone and his flesh, and he will curse thee to thy face" (v. 5). Here too, the Lord accepts the devil's provocation, and the following verse grants his wish: "Behold, he is in your power; only spare his life," just as he had previously placed limits on touching his person.

We know the story well. Job remains faithful to his Lord despite all the calamities and the myriad doubts which the devil instills in him through the people near him, his wife and his friends. When Satan is given his lesson, God restores to Job his health, his fortunes, and all his possessions, multiplying them even. *Just like Job, man's fidelity attains the fourfold aim of humiliating the devil (the Accuser in the book of Revelation), of giving praise to God, receiving his recompense, and participating in the redemption of the world.*

On the other hand, an episode from the Gospel comes to mind: that of the rich young man (Matt. 19:16–22). He is the one who goes to the Master to learn the path of holiness. His request is noble, because his moral conduct is already lofty. In his confession to Jesus, the young man explains how he already observes all the commandments and the law of Abraham. Jesus reads his soul and knows he is sincere. In the Gospels of Mark and Luke, He expresses Himself clearly: "And Jesus looking upon him loved him." Then He responded to his question, pointing out the path of perfect holiness and total dedication to God: "If you would be perfect, go, sell what you possess and give to the poor, and you will have treasure in heaven; and come, follow me." Jesus proposes to him a final leap, but he is not able to renounce the ease and powers of wealth. Jesus loves him in that moment and would like God to be everything for him. But the one who could take that leap, because it was within his ability, refused the proposal.

Of course, we do not know how it ended. We can imagine that the rich young man eventually freed himself of this last weakness of his, that he eventually chose the path of Zaccheus or the faithful servant in the parable, making a return on his investment through love and respect for the One who had entrusted him with his wealth. We only know that Jesus turned to the disciples who witnessed the scene and said that terrible and famous line: "Truly, I say to you, it will be hard for a rich man to enter the kingdom of heaven. Again I tell you, it is easier for a camel to go through the eye of a needle than for a rich man to enter the kingdom of God."

Such a harsh expression. The disciples perceive that the concept of riches implies all that keeps one tied to the world and they are disturbed. For this reason, they ask, "Who then can be saved?" *Jesus' answer is pure light, capable of instilling great hope into our lives: "With men this is impossible, but with God all things are possible." Such a great hope that an even greater certainty is added: "Every one who has left houses or brothers or sisters or father or mother or children or lands, for my name's sake, will receive a hundredfold, and inherit eternal life. But many that are first will be last, and the last first."*

An interesting passage from St. Paul (2 Cor. 12:7–10) clarifies the motives for which God allows the devil to intervene in the lives of the elect: "To keep me from being too elated by the abundance of revelations, a thorn was given me in the flesh, a messenger of Satan, to harass me, to keep me from being too elated. Three times I besought the Lord about this, that it should leave me; but he said to me, 'My grace is sufficient for you, for my power is made perfect in weakness.' I will all the more gladly boast of my weaknesses, that the power of Christ may rest upon me. For the sake of Christ, then, I am content with weaknesses, insults, hardships, persecutions, and calamities; for when I am weak, then I am strong."

In light of this reasoning on temptations, also with reference to the young rich man, we must remember the general rule that the devil is never allowed to afflict a person beyond their ability to resist the pain or the flattery of temptations. The saints at the highest level, normal people at the lowest level. And if they were to fall, it is always due to their free will that they let themselves go, following their weaknesses.

According to St. Francis's first biographer and confrere Thomas of Celano, St. Francis explained to one of his friars who was suffering a temptation, "Believe me, my son, for this reason I consider you a servant of God, and that you might know that the more you are tempted, the more you are dear to me. No one should consider himself a servant of God if he has not experienced temptations and tribulations. Temptation, overcome in a proper manner, is the ring by which the Lord espouses the soul of his servant. Many are satisfied with the merits acquired over many years and rejoice at not having experienced any sort of temptation; we know, however, that this is an indication that the Lord has considered them spiritually weak, since even before the battle they were terrified of winning it. In fact, intense combat will not arise for those without the strength of soul to withstand it."

Just like St. Francis exhorted his brothers, so too did the venerable Maria Giuseppina of Jesus Crucified, a Discalced Carmelite and foundress in Naples of the Monastery of Saints Joseph and Teresa, remind her sisters of the mission they had chosen at the moment of their entrance into the cloister with these words: "A nun is a soul who closes herself into the cloister as a soldier in the trenches to wage combat. You, therefore, must realize you are in Carmel for the defense of souls against the assaults of the infernal enemy. Do not grieve, then, over the interior struggle you suffer and that grows within you, instead of the peace and quiet which you had dreamed of. Remember that this is the office of the soul consecrated to our blessed God: to fight and to win." St. Catherine of Siena said that God allows the devil to persecute us "to provide us the means for meriting, as well as to rouse us from the slumber of acedia."

The devil is capable of causing enormous suffering to one who undertakes the path of sanctity. And the saints, through their fidelity to God, contribute to the final triumph of good, and to the redeeming work of Jesus. It is easy to remember the example of Padre Pio. The devil tried everything on him, from temptations, to physical pain, to blows. And Padre Pio, with the same pride of faith that St. Paul had, was able to say: "I have always won."

How to Hire a Murderer

The second of the devil's direct interventions that can be termed "not culpable" or "innocent" for the one suffering it is the curse or evil spell. *This is the main cause of the actions without attributable guilt, and although it is rare, it produces evils that are the worst for the person, at least in appearance.*

Concretely, a curse is described as the maleficent action of one person against another carried out by the devil. We must not forget that the devil cannot act directly against man but only through human mediation. Essentially, the devil can be accepted by a free choice or can be suffered insofar as someone has hurled him against you, has put a curse on you in other words. Something that is terrible and devastating just to think of. *It's like hiring a hitman, or a gang of thugs or aggressors.*

In the face of this seemingly unavoidable evil, however, it is good to remember *that curses can do nothing to a person united to God in prayer and who has made a precise choice in life in favor of Christ. A choice we are called to renew daily for ourselves and for the people dear to us, in our prayers and in our daily actions.* And it is not merely conditioning if our thoughts go to the answer of the crowd to Pilate's question (Matt. 27:17): "Who do you want me to release for you, Barabbas or Jesus who is called Christ?"

More than 95 percent of cases of possession or evils caused by the devil (much more frequent than possessions) are due to curses. There are many types of curses. They have been used since time immemorial and continue to be practiced with the same means: spells, charms, the evil eye, slurs, hexes, Macumba, voodoo, and potions, just to name a few. These words call to mind ages and beliefs one thought to be buried at the dawn of time. In reality, these are ongoing practices. Just look into the arsenal of any magician or witch to understand that these things have not gone out of fashion.

It is important to clarify that the victim who suffers the curse is innocent. The effects of the curse they have been afflicted with cannot be attributed to them. Even if we are dealing with a person possessed by the devil. On the other hand, "gravely culpable" (Fr. Amorth uses precisely this expression to define the extreme degree of guilt) *is the one who performs the curse and who commissions the devil. These are people who act on behalf of the devil or who have placed themselves in the hands of the devil to obtain their objectives. To expiate such wickedness a radical change of life is necessary: constant prayer, exercise of charity, and the sincere frequenting of the sacrament of Confession. Without this, the harm caused to the victims cannot be rectified, at least in most cases.*

There are many stories, all of them quite disturbing because they are often tied to the close affections of the person afflicted. *One who performs a curse or commissions it is often the parent, a relative, an in-law, or an intimate friend of the one stricken. And it is precisely in the area of close affective relationships that one finds the most difficult cases.* It is as if the hatred with which the curse is made were directly proportionate to the strength of the prior affective bond, and with that strength one lashes out on the person.

Fr. Candido told the story of a daughter of a rural couple, a poor family that put their daughter through college with great sacrifices. Her parents interpreted her graduation as the beginning of an important step up the social ladder and placed in her all their ambitions and desires to redeem and vindicate themselves. They were terribly disappointed when she fell in love with a factory worker and told them of their relationship.

Her parents fought their relationship in every way. The young couple stayed together, and their bond grew stronger thanks to this adversity.

When they announced their intention to get married, it seemed to the girl that her mother and father had begun to resign themselves. She spoke to her fiancé, and both were delighted. The wedding date was set and they began preparations. They thought everything was going smoothly. They did not realize, however, that the original disapproval in the heart of her parents had matured into profound hatred that was waiting for the right time to show itself fully. The wedding took place regularly in church. The guests went to the restaurant for the wedding feast. At a certain point during the banquet, her father called her aside into another room of the restaurant and there, with words prepared in great detail and with absolute satanic malice, cursed her, her husband, their union, and their eventual children, guaranteeing them the worst evils. From that moment, the two newlyweds began an endless Calvary. The husband lost his job. Sickness and disasters of every sort followed one after another. Such was the wickedness with which the curse had been made that Fr. Candido was never able to resolve the case, but could only bring about partial benefits.

There are also curses that are renewed systematically. I have seen cases in which the one who made the curse learned about the exorcisms of their victims and every time repeated the rite of the curse. In these cases, however, if there is assiduous prayer and exorcisms, it can be said that the curse usually weakens, although much time is needed for liberation. It can be said that this is the classic type of curse in which, if the instigator dies, liberation becomes simpler. This is the opposite of cases of very strong curses in which, despite the death or sincere repentance of the instigator, liberation remains difficult. I remember a mother who cursed her son and then repented of it and began an arduous path of faith and expiation. But her efforts were not enough to liberate her son from diabolical influence.

We must remember that previously the Church held that exorcisms ought only to be applied to those under demonic possession. The current catechism has taken a great step forward, however, underlining that even in cases of diabolical influence the exorcism should be performed. And cases of curses with diabolical influences are relatively frequent.

It is enough to follow the work of an exorcist for a few days to realize this. His appointment book is always full. And the cases often seem to be the same, one after another. Sentiments of hatred and jealousy are focused on the very same things and strike, when possible, the affections, money, work, success, beauty, health, and the home they live in.

There are examples of homes afflicted by curses, with noises, lights, and appliances that turn on, rendering peaceful sleep impossible. People in such conditions suffer terribly. And liberating a home from a curse is very difficult. Quite often, one is forced to invite the inhabitants to move. It can also happen that other reasons for these events are discovered: that a suicide has occurred in the house, or fortune tellers or magicians or members of satanic cults had lived there previously; or that seances have taken place there, or heinous murderers lived there, or summary executions took place within it or outside it (there are many stories of cursed houses tied to terrible episodes that occurred in periods of war); or that the land on which the house was built was an old cemetery, with deceased who have not found eternal peace.

But there can also be more common factors, because really, every type of wickedness stubbornly sought out and obtained can produce similar situations, even though usually it is caused by the spiritual or psychological disturbances of the people concerned. Thus, blessing the home or moving to another is entirely useless. The problem is within us and must be resolved within us: above all through forgiveness and entrusting oneself to Mary and to Divine Mercy.

Since the early centuries, Christians have been aware of the possibility that the devil can take possession and enter not only human beings but also animals and objects. The Gospel guides us in this matter, for example, with the emblematic case of the exorcism of the Gerasene demoniac, and the demons that entered the swine. The Church Fathers were quick to analyze these things. Origen openly testified that in the name of Jesus one can cast out demons present not only in people, but also in objects, houses, and animals. The *Catechism of the Catholic Church* makes this explicit in paragraph 1673, where it defines the meaning of exorcism: "When the Church asks publicly and authoritatively in the name of Jesus Christ that a person or object be protected against the power of the Evil One and withdrawn from his dominion, it is called *exorcism*."

We must be careful to interpret the phenomena concerning persons and animals correctly. At times there have been obvious misunderstandings. An amusing case happened to Don Bosco. He once went into a house in the countryside to spend some days resting. He was with a few other people. During the night they started hearing loud noises coming from the roof that seemed inexplicable. He thought it might be the presence of demons, because he had often been afflicted by them. He began to pray. Then, noticing that the noises did not stop, he decided to have a look with his friends, and found a hen that had gotten stuck in the attic and fluttered about terrorized. To celebrate the positive and hilarious outcome of that sleepless night, they killed the hen, plucked out its feathers, and ate it.

One wonders why curses are so relatively widespread. *The spirit of revenge, the desire to get back at others, hatred, malice for malice's sake are all very common and absurd evils, although doing such things gains nothing. We have an innate tendency to evil that we struggle to keep under control and the devil is continually on the lookout for each of our weak points. If, instead of resisting him, flying from temptations by entrusting ourselves in prayer to divine protection, we gravitate toward evil and go looking for it to procure it for others, then one truly offers the devil his opportunity, not only to instigate our actions, but also to project outward the evil that we so obstinately demand.*

Magicians, Witches, and Fortune Tellers

Among the "culpable" causes of the devil's intervention in the life of a person is frequenting magicians and fortune tellers. This is a very widespread phenomenon that has become even more common ever since television was transformed into an efficacious instrument of persuasion. For many local TV stations, and not only them, to sell airtime to magicians and fortune tellers is business comparable to any other advertising — greater than the diffusion of pornographic films, and very similar, in terms of profits, to the promotion of erotic telephone numbers. Above all, it's an easy business because, as always, evil requires no effort. Entire time slots are bought by these people, who through the television can multiply their exposure to vulnerable people, many of whom have little spiritual depth and can be easily duped. This is the same logic that justifies, in the minds of media companies, allotting whole swaths of programming to the showgirls promoting erotic telephone hotlines. The result is always the same: corrupt people make money through the corruption of other people. The spiritual consequences, naturally, vary from person to person, from magician to magician, or from showgirl to showgirl.

The environment frequented by magicians is populated by the most disparate types of human beings, including men and women who often have difficulty in their relationship with the sacred, in particular with the Catholic Faith. Many of them are well-educated, even important people who consult magicians or who have their cards read or their horoscope foreseen. There are also great numbers of secularists, always ready to criticize as inane the truths of the faith, but who do not disdain frequenting these haunts. One setting that is difficult not to include in the list of the adherents, although only formally, is that of people who have become absorbed in Eastern religion and philosophy, in the pantheism of New Age spirituality, or presumed forms of clairvoyance, such as those linked to millenarist beliefs or mysterious, incomprehensible writings. Around such things a rich media and commercial web has been spun: films, programs, TV and radio personalities, books, magazines, gadgets, advertising, and other products of mass consumption.

It must be said of magicians, fortune tellers, and clairvoyants that most of them are charlatans. Their only interest is to drain their victims of their money. Their "diabolic" intentions, if this term can be used in the sense of cunning employed at deceiving and fleecing people, is limited to this alone. Although this too comes with serious consequences, because many people who are taken in by them end up impoverished, along with their families. One must also consider that in some ways, their actions, which take advantage of the spiritual distress of people and their ignorance of the truth, are an extension of the devil's main activity: distancing people from God, corrupting them, and leading them to perdition.

The question of magicians with real power derived from their diabolical activities is entirely different. And it does not matter if it is black magic or so-called white magic. One must be suspicious in all cases, because every power that does not come directly from God comes from the evil one. We are speaking, of course, of magicians, but also witches, wizards, and sorceresses. These are obsolete terms, but in this case they are to be understood in their original meaning as people who act as a vehicle for evil, who receive from evil the powers by which they make their proselytes, from whom curses can be commissioned.

There are many types. Some are particularly capable in their media impact on their clients, others are crude to the point of arousing wonder at their ability to gain their confidence, and still others do not even seem to be on the market, but hiddenly act with equal effectiveness on their own behalf or on behalf of others. Within this vast gamut of external traits, *their actions have been the same as in past centuries and millennia. Their actions, gestures, and the materials they use take one back in time to the darkest meanders of history and of perversion. A dark world made up of concoctions, spells, rites, invocations, magical powers and potions, toads, mice, serpents, black cats, hairpins, cloth dolls, clotted blood, menstrual blood, rusty nails, strange metallic forms, and so forth.*

By means of these objects and animals they carry out their evil rites on commission. And there should be no doubt about their effectiveness. Through them, the devil works directly on the people to whom the curses are directed, and if one does not lead a life of faith, by the daily abandonment to Providence, sustained by prayer, through the communion of saints and devotion to the Virgin Mary, it will be difficult to resist. The same thing can be said for what happens afterward, once these evils have afflicted the person, because besides the particularly serious cases in which exorcisms are needed, one is liberated from these things through prayer, the assiduous recourse to the sacraments, invocation of divine grace, and pilgrimage to sanctuaries. A simple malign influence, if it is not perceived as such, can slowly parch our soul and invariably lead us down the path of evil.

For a Plate of Eggplant

When someone comes to me saying he has consulted a magician, I ask him if he was offered anything to eat or drink. One must always suspect something malicious.

Here we are in the world of the apparently impossible. The stories we are preparing to tell seem truly impossible, if not actually the fruit of some horror fantasy or some screenwriter with mental and spiritual disturbances. And these are the least horrid tales. The problem is, they truly occurred, and for this reason must be considered so we can understand fully the abyss of diabolical perversions. *The devil is not interested in how; he is only interested in the result.* And when the how is presented in all its unfathomable ugliness and maleficence, it truly captures the reality of the matter.

Evil, beyond its varying degrees and initial appearances, is always ugly and malicious. *For this reason, I always tell parents, teachers, and priests that we must educate children to love the beautiful from their earliest years. And I am not the only one who says this: in the lives and sayings of many saints this admonition turns up everywhere.* Not only because the beautiful draws us closer to the mystical vision of God, and in this the Gospel account of the Transfiguration can be helpful, but also because familiarity with the beautiful, with its most intimate essence, increases in us the instinct to defend ourselves from all that can cause us material and spiritual harm.

In this type of situation, perspicacity is one's first line of defense. And if one is watchful in the sense described just now, one also participates in the spiritual defense that Jesus Christ, the Virgin Mary, our guardian angel, and our patron saints are ready to provide for us. Evil can, in fact, take us by surprise. *Unfortunately, at times the people we least expect are the ones who do these things, and in the ways we could least imagine. After years of exorcisms, for example, a man suffering from evil curses for having eaten a plate of eggplant is finally being liberated.*

It all started when he was eight years old and a relative had him eat a dish made with eggplant on which he had put a curse out of pure envy and malice. Thirty years later it's as if he had just eaten the cursed dish. He can still taste it in his mouth with a reflux and stomach pain. When he goes to the bathroom, he defecates as if he had just eaten eggplant, though he has never eaten it since that time, nor can he bear to hear eggplant spoken of, since he began to suffer the effects of that curse immediately.

I recently had to reprimand severely a person I know who had gone to a friend whom she knew was dedicated to magic and in this woman's house had drunk a cup of coffee she had kindly offered her. From her account of the matter, it was immediately clear that there had been a malicious attempt. She had her sit down in the living room and brought out from the kitchen two cups already filled with coffee. "This is for you," she said. When she reached for the one cup, the woman repeated with gentle firmness that hers was the other cup. And my friend, not wanting to displease her host by refusing, drank the coffee. I told her she had incurred a grave risk. She should never have accepted.

Usually, these people offer you the most common things. Often it is a cup of coffee, chocolates taken from a box that is already open. At times, it is a piece of cake already cut into pieces. In all cases, food and drink in which it is possible to dissolve substances or insert them without noticing their presence.

What do they use? As we have already explained, the materials are the same as from the dawn of time. If I must add to the list some substances of which I have had direct experience, I would add powder of ground human bone, pulverized menstrual blood, the blood of certain animals such as toads. I have even looked for an explanation about why these substances in particular. What I can say is that if they continue to use these ancient rituals it is because they have been discovered to have an evil efficacy through some agreement with the devil.

At any rate, it is logical to consider that bones have an intrinsic symbolism of death, and that they might have belonged to a person who while living had made a pact with Satan or was even killed in a satanic ritual. These observations explain the reason for the mysterious profanations of graves we occasionally hear about. *The reason for menstrual blood I believe depends on the fact that it is something tied to nascent life and therefore, by diabolical opposition, can give rise to death.*

Concerning toads, I have often noticed their use without understanding the real motive. What can be said is that the toad, by nature innocent (as was the eggplant in the previous story), is associated with ugliness, and therefore is often to be found in stories tied to magic. In my experience, I remember two very peculiar accounts, though quite distinct in their outcomes.

An exorcist friend told me about a woman he never saw again, who brought him a toad in a closed bag with water in it. Certainly odd. He gave little notice to it, in part because so many strange people come to us exorcists afflicted by a range of oddities, but also because he saw no harm in the animal. Distracted by other tasks, he had not even thought about freeing it. After a brief interview, he took leave of the woman and put the sack on a chair thinking he would deal with it later. After a few hours, he remembered the sack and went to get it. It was on the same chair, closed as before with all the water in it, but the toad had vanished. No one had entered his house. The floor was dry under the chair, and despite the windows and doors being closed, the toad was nowhere to be found. What is certain is that the eventual malicious intentions of the woman who had brought it into my friend's house had had no effect whatsoever.

Toads, Snakes, and Rusty Nails

QUITE DIFFERENT WAS THE *incident that happened to Fr. Candido in the 1970s. A boy had been cursed by a woman connected to the devil, a witch who put spells on people for money and whom everyone in that area knew. This boy, a peasant who had always enjoyed good health, began to waste away physically. From one day to the next, he became thinner and weaker. The doctors could not remedy his problem. Medical tests could not identify the cause. Medicine had no effect. Knowing the witch by name, Fr. Candido had gone to her on occasion seeking information. Fortunately, she had a weakness for money and, when paid enough, she told how she had put the spell on him. She had taken a toad and placed it in a hole where it could barely move, and where it could not eat. Then she tied the fate of that peasant boy to that of the toad. The more the toad wasted away, the more the boy did, too. When the woman finally pointed out where the animal was to be found, they went looking for it, found it, and liberated it. It was about to die, but once it was in the open and could eat, it began to recover. The boy began to recover too, and returned to normal life. As odd as it seemed, it was immediately clear to everyone that if the toad had died, there would have been no chance for the boy.*

Another question concerns people under a curse who find the strangest objects in mattresses and pillows. *They must be blessed, then burnt in the open while praying intensely. And it is important that they be burnt far from the home of the person to whom the curse was directed. Once it took more than two canisters of gasoline to burn one such mattress stuffed with horsehair. It didn't want to be burned.*

Such events are quite common among the people who come for the exorcisms. When they and the people accompanying them tell me before undergoing the rite what they have gone through since the last meeting, I always ask them not to leave out the least element. Everything can be useful to the exorcist for understanding the nature of the evil, whether there has been a deterioration, or whether they are moving toward liberation. At times these people bring common objects in which they have noticed something strange, objects given to them by random strangers never seen again. People have brought pillows, blankets, or mattresses in which strange stains suddenly appear or strange substances are detected within.

And to think that I did not want to believe the experience of a friend's family, regarding a big rusty nail that an elderly relative had found several decades earlier inside her woolen mattress, which she usually combed and refreshed herself, while finding no hole or sign of tampering on the outside. This phenomenon was explained by the presence of a perverse witch in a neighboring home in the countryside. Even the owner of the mattress, although she did not live in prosperity and to whom wool had always been considered valuable to the point of constantly recycling it, decided to burn it on a bonfire, accompanying the fire with prayers.

When they told me this story, on one side I gave it little importance, but on the other it seemed a relic of superstitions tied to rural and rustic people. Then I witnessed similar phenomena with my own eyes, and I had no more doubts.

These are not matters that are inserted manually into mattresses, but rather they appear there via malevolent means. The case of rusty nails is a frequent one. Often they are pieces of iron twisted together. At times they take the form of animals. Very often there are big clots of blood balled up, pieces of plastic also. The experiences of many exorcists even mention living animals. Once I happened to find a living snake in the mattress of a person I had been exorcising for some time, and who often had nocturnal disturbances. None of us was objectively able to say how it had gotten inside there and remained alive.

Those sleeping on such mattresses and pillows are immediately aware that something has changed. They start complaining of physical disturbances of every sort, pain in their head and stomach, illnesses, insomnia, nightmares. If they tell this to a prudent priest or to an exorcist they will likely be immediately suspect. Then they ask questions to understand better. Often it is enough simply to ascertain if those symptoms appear when they sleep for a certain period somewhere else. At times they are advised to do a weeklong spiritual retreat. If the symptoms disappear, then it is likely that the problem is connected to the place of residence. It might be their home, a neighbor, or even just the mattress or pillow.

The Devil? Tell Me Where He Is Not

One must be very cautious of magicians and of all those who dabble in the magical arts and any form of prediction of the future, just as a prudent person must be very wary of any other form of culpable dabbling with the demonic. We are talking about precise, conscious choices in favor of such involvement.

We will return to the extraordinary activity of the devil in the life of men in a moment. Here it is important to note that we are all subject, from birth to death, in the most banal aspects of our daily life, to the ordinary activity of the devil.

One time, a man in a city in Northern Italy, where I went for a conference, criticized me, saying, "Fr. Amorth, you see the devil everywhere."

I responded without losing my calm: "Tell me where he is not."

The Gospel episodes witnessing the daily presence of the devil are many. Take the first chapter of Mark and you see this, considering that it was the first to be given written form and therefore the most closely tied to the events narrated. Many scholars think it was written first in Aramaic, a consideration that seems confirmed when one realizes that the Greek translation is perfectly adapted to the styles and forms of that language.

Well, in the first chapter of Mark, the daily relationship between man and the devil is presented clearly. After the temptation in the desert, Jesus liberates a man possessed by a demon. Then he liberates others who are possessed and sends the apostles out to liberate those possessed by demons. In the Gospel of John (particularly loved and studied by many theologians today), not one exorcism is narrated, although the devil is continually mentioned, both his works and his power. He is called "the prince of this world," who by Jesus' actions will be "cast out" (12:31). In John 8:44, it says that the devil "was a murderer from the beginning, and has nothing to do with the truth, because there is no truth in him. When he lies, he speaks according to his own nature, for he is a liar and the father of lies." In John 7:7, Jesus emphasizes, "The world cannot hate you, but it hates me because I testify of it that its works are evil." It is a concept of the world which in John is often repeated and given the meaning of whatever opposes Jesus, contrasts his work, and seeks his death. According to this logic, John repeats in his First Letter that "the entire world is under the power of the evil one" and that "Jesus has come to defeat the works of Satan." From such affirmations one can safely deduce that those who do not believe in the existence of Satan can easily not believe in Jesus' existence, who came to establish the Kingdom of God in the place of that of the devil. In this regard, we must remember that St. Paul, with the same logic of opposition, calls the devil "the god of this world."

The devil is so rooted in this world that the sacred texts go so far as to identify him with the world itself. Following the Gospel of John, one understands that Jesus' actions are in opposition to the world — a world that always and everywhere seeks to corrupt his disciples just as it sought to corrupt him. All men are subject to the constant action of the evil one.

People often ask me if even the Virgin Mary was tempted. Of course, I respond, she was tempted her entire life, but she always triumphed over Satan's attempts. During exorcisms, demons often openly denounce their sense of defeat in the face of the Virgin Mary. They are angry with her and fear her because she vanquished them, and always will.

In one of the apparitions at Medjugorje, it was Mary herself who emphasized that the devil is everywhere, and even more so where she manifests her presence. "When I go somewhere [in other words, when an apparition occurs] Jesus is always with me, but the devil is always rushing behind." In the sanctuaries, the places of the apparitions, and the places made famous by the presence and works of the saints, the devil is quite present and always seeks to work on people's hearts and minds. For example, I notice he is very active when we celebrate particular functions for healing and liberation. His aim is to render them ineffective. Every healing and liberation is a defeat for him. We exorcists must be very careful at times about who participates, because there are people who come to us only to destroy and come for Communion only to profane it. For this reason, we are very strict about the invitations. Deception lies around every corner. If one were to go to a magician or a fortune teller, to give an example, one often finds them surrounded by sacred images of every sort, but that is only to trick poor souls. It is the deception of Satan.

And certainly not only magicians want to deceive us. All society is woven with deceit, and one must know how to untangle oneself from this with great care. As it says in the Gospel, the purity of the dove must be paired with the cunning of the snake. To every deception there corresponds real human drama. One encounters it on every corner. *Because the current pervasiveness and presence of the evil one has no equal in history.* Of course, we must not despair, because the victories of evil over humanity are always temporary, precarious, and can be immediately overturned. History, at any rate, belongs to God, and it is enough to recognize His great plan to triumph over the devil.

At the same time, we must be realistic and not hide behind false utopias. The devil is active like never before and the main causes of his widespread presence in our society are evident. First, there is the progressive de-Christianization that has now reached its final stage, of entire nations, in particular those which historically bore the destinies of Christianity such as France, Spain, Austria, and Italy. We have witnessed a process of religious crisis and infiltration of evil into the habits of individuals and gradually into ideologies, customs, and laws. Once the Decalogue is removed, every sort of aberration is justifiable. Consciences have been corrupted as much as the seas and the sky have been polluted.

Along with this problem there is discouragement, degradation, the ever-decreasing appeal of the clergy and religious life in general. There are fewer and fewer priests. A great many of them are not wholly dedicated to their pastoral work, just as they dedicated less and less time to the sacrament of Penance. There is a growing ethical relativism among them influenced by cultural models proposed by the world. Their spiritual life is simply not contagious. They believe less and less in the devil and his works, often not denying his existence outright, but acting as if he didn't exist. In a word, they are increasingly distant from the real needs of men, less of an example than ever, and less helpful than ever. And the scandals that frequently crash against the entire ecclesial community, at times even within the Vatican, must be seen as the perverse fruit of these attitudes. The devil is intensely interested in insinuating himself in the Church, even at the highest levels, as history teaches. If he succeeds in creeping into a crack, he does all he can to transform it into a crevice. And yet, in recent decades, we have had popes who have been very careful to indicate to religious and priests the radicality of the struggle against the evil one. John Paul II often spoke of the devil and his works. He performed exorcisms. During his many journeys, he sat in the confessional to reaffirm to priests and the faithful the fundamental importance of the sacrament of Reconciliation. The teaching of Benedict XVI on the evil one was always clear, inviting the faithful to wage a fierce war and explicitly encouraging exorcists in their difficult ministry in the service of the Church.

The exorcist Msgr. Andrea Gemma, archbishop emeritus of Isernia-Venafro, expressed himself in an interview with *Petrus* on January 8, 2008, concerning Benedict XVI and the difficult battle he had to confront against evil. He told of an exorcism he had to perform a few hours after the election of Cardinal Joseph Ratzinger to the papal throne. The devil, speaking through the mouth of the woman he was exorcising, said, "This is a tragedy, Benedict XVI is even stronger, even worse than John Paul II." Msgr. Gemma immediately added that these words did not surprise him at all, because "Cardinal Ratzinger had always fought the devil and warned humanity of his dangers."

The third fundamental question is the perverse use of the media, which can dictate customs and form moral behaviors. This is something entirely unheard of before in all history. And the near total dedication of the media to the principles of evil is a logical consequence of the two previous causes. The Virgin Mary foresaw this in Fátima, that scandalous customs would become common. From that moment there has been a crescendo capable of devastating entire peoples in the brief span of a generation.

Just watch the television, or go to a movie, or browse the web, and you can see the behavior of young people, their language, their dress, and their increasingly violent habits, disrespectful of sex and life. Fashion is, from this point of view, a primary vehicle of the new moral attitudes. The fact that the sexual behavior of so many fashion designers is modeled on the pervasive logic of every sort of vice has led to it being poured into the manner of dress and the ways of caring for the body of the new generations, with an increasingly evanescent distinction between what is masculine and what is feminine. Not to mention a certain type of aggressive and violent clothing and an even more subtle diffusion of T-shirts, shoes, hats, and jackets covered with designs, labels, and writing that invoke the devil in all his names and meanings.

The same could be said as regards the systematic corruption carried out by the media with respect to the family, relations between men and women, between parents and children, and even between grandparents and grandchildren. The family, and all that has kept it together in the West, has suffered a violent attack at the hands of literature, television, cinema, advertising, news programs, comics, and the Internet.

Even magazines specializing in home furnishings have taken care to remove Jesus Christ and the Virgin Mary from families. The practical demonstration of this is quite simple to demonstrate: take any of these publications, whatever the editor, and see if, in the furnishings for bedrooms and living rooms or in the pictures of the beautiful homes showcased, there appears even one sacred image. Every painting, every object, even the oddest, is fine for decorating a bedroom, but never a crucifix or an image of Mary. Lit candles and New Age symbols are never lacking, or illustrations taken from Eastern religions, not to mention drawings or graphics that recall the esoteric.

All this goes to show that beyond the increasingly widespread spiritualistic, occult, and satanic practices, there is vast evidence of events, habits, and trends that we cannot automatically define as blameworthy or innocent according to the definitions given above, but which in some way can open the doors to the intervention of the evil one in our lives. In almost every case, the issue is connected to the lifestyle of the moment, to typical habits of society, to certain forms of entertainment that often, though not in their essence, assume the traits of downright witches' sabbaths and initiation rites. *These issues must be approached with great prudence. These situations, in fact, are not necessarily tied to the evil one. Most of the time, it has nothing to do with him, but are merely convincing simulations or simply imitations. We do well to act always with prudence and to avoid them, if possible, and to warn our children and young friends to avoid them, because it is especially the younger generations, less cautious in the face of evil, who run the greater risk of not being able to distinguish between real entertainment and perversion. And increasingly what is being proposed as entertainment is only perversion.*

Halloween Witches

The feast of All Saints was just around the corner. The third-grade son of a friend returned from school and gave his mother an invitation to a party on the afternoon of October 31. The woman, whose religious convictions would not have allowed her son to attend any Halloween party anyway, was amazed when she read the invitation. It was a full sheet of paper, with an image downloaded from the Internet on it and folded twice so that the invitation had four sides to it. On the first were two pumpkins with the classical nose, mouth, and two black cats, with the writing: "You are invited to the most spectral and gloomy Halloween Party ever."

On the fourth side was a horrible image of Leonardo's Mona Lisa in black garb with a black background, toothless, and her face and hands skin and bones. Complete ugliness. A sort of appetizer of the spectral and the lugubrious announced on the front side, with the subtlety of an image connected to an occultist Leonardo, so dear to recent bestsellers, nearly blasphemous to some, and certainly animated by an anti-Christian spirit.

The best part (or worst, we might say) came when the woman read the two internal sides and found an invitation to an actual witch's sabbath.

On one side was written: "We look forward to spending with you an evening full of amusement. We await your confirmation to inform the netherworld of your coming."

Following this were the date, hour, and address where the party was being held. Then, on the third side, in red, with a clumsy attempt at poetry and seemingly playful expression, the invitation continued to the point of near delirium: "Gliding down from the sky are many old witches, with their curved noses, their beards, and their hats. They are coming and gathering to celebrate tonight. Beware, don't sleep, don't miss the best part! If they offer you a potion during the rites and the magic, take it and certainly you'll have lots to do! Go for a ride with them on their brooms. Take a ride into the dark and gloomy night."

It's not hard to imagine how those two parents, upon reading this, became even more convinced in their opposition to Halloween. That invitation had been written by a thirteen-year-old boy, already capable of understanding how certain things work, finding phrases and downloading images here and there from the Internet, and constructing a satanic rite — which certainly did not take place, but it's enough to consider it to make a prudent person shiver.

Their son was invited to RSVP so that someone in the netherworld might better prepare to welcome him. And a father and a mother with common sense would certainly not allow their child to go somewhere where they await him in the netherworld. And nothing about it gave the impression that they were joking, because one can have fun in a thousand other ways that are less "mortiferous," because we have heard of many pranks like this that come to a bad end and perhaps have even had direct experience of some of these sad events.

The child was invited to drink a potion, moreover. Now, leaving aside the saying that you should never accept candy from strangers, given that a thirteen-year-old child is no longer a little one, one must ask how parents would allow their child to go freely to a party where consuming mysterious "substances" has been announced as an extraordinary experience. And placing the concept of substance in quotation marks was not fortuitous. We know all too well how easy it is in clubs for drugs to be mixed into drinks and served with the intent to deceive.

Not to mention that it is precisely thanks to the "substances" consumed that one "gets down to work," as the invitation recited, taking part in activities whose consequences can be permanent. Not to mention the cases in which those "substances" place one under the influence of the "witches" or "wizards" of the day. Not, finally, to mention the invitation "to go for a ride," which seems the equivalent of the notion of a drug trip.

All of this before entering the even darker world of witches, the real ones, and their magical potions of which we have already spoken. In that world, the gates of Hell are truly opened, as happened in the following two episodes narrated on the eve of All Saints in the newspaper of the Italian Episcopal Conference, *Avvenire,* by Fr. Aldo Buonaiuto, director of the office for cults and the occult of the Association of Pope John XXIII, who also happens to be an auxiliary of the Judicial Police and consultant of the judiciary. These episodes were verified during interviews with the victims by the journalist Pino Ciociola. The setting was two cities in Northern Italy.

"Recently, I have found myself wandering the streets unable to remember my name, where I came from, and what I was doing there. I have been through so much evil, sex, drugs, and violence that I don't want to talk about it." This was the story of Leonardo, a teenager who was considered "young, very young," the story of one who was "torn to pieces in body and soul" by satanic malice.

It all began when "outside my school I saw a poster advertising a Halloween party and a free course for becoming a witch hunter." At 11:30 on that October 31, Leonardo arrived at the party with his friends. Everyone was wearing costumes. "The music was great.

Mannequins were dangling from the ceiling like hanged men, as well as bloody bats. The chairs were decorated like skeletons. On the walls you could see portraits of serial killers and Charles Manson.... There were different ways of transgressing, either with the substances that were going around or in the excitement in the air, sexual as well." It was an evening that the boy called "fun and exciting." Then the owner of the club approached him along with a few others and asked if they wanted to take the course mentioned on the poster.

Of course, no adolescent would take seriously the phrase "witch hunter." At any rate, a few days later Leonardo called them: "They gave me an address close to home, so I went." The address corresponded to an apartment. He was received by a woman who took his name, telephone number, and address. Prudent people: first they get informed about who they are dealing with, about the families, then they choose the most gullible kids, the most harmless. Some days later, Leonardo was contacted. In the apartment he found five other kids his age, three boys and three girls. A woman gave them a lesson on the symbolism of Halloween centered on "all the cosmic energies of the universe with great positive and esoteric potentiality." The six adolescents found this discussion fascinating, and the woman was so convincing that she was able to reproduce the same atmosphere they had experienced in the nightclub. She convinced them that they were the "privileged ones," who "belong to the god Samhain," that what they are doing is a "school of energy," and that "a new life" was opening up before them in which they could fulfill "all their dreams and all their pleasures." At a certain point, the woman said out loud, "Nothing and no one will be able to stop you from fulfilling your desires."

From that day on, Leonardo frequented the group once a week, under obligation to keep the matter secret so as not to risk losing all his powers. "At first I liked it." Then, "they forced me to hate everyone: parents, relatives, teachers. I tried to run away from home four times. They put it into my head that only the school of energy could understand me and resolve my problems. I suffered so much evil." It was his parents who pulled him out of it. At a certain point, they realized their son was in difficulty and took him to the hospital. "There, the reconstruction of my life and my psyche began." His last words in the interview were an accusation, emphasizing in strong terms the educational emergency that is strangling our society: "I hope everyone understands that there needs to be greater vigilance on the part of parents and teachers, so that what happened to me does not happen to others."

The obligation is to be vigilant, to be present, to teach the biblical texts with greater emphasis. At the beginning of the fourth chapter of Deuteronomy, Moses explains that abiding by the law one becomes an example, because there are no gods as close to their people "as the Lord our God is near to us whenever we invoke him" and there are no laws and rules as just as those of our Lord. But he warns: "Take heed, and keep your soul diligently, lest you forget the things your eyes have seen, and lest they depart from your heart all the days of your life, make them known to your children and your children's children."

The second story concerns a young couple. At the time the events took place, three years before the story was told, she was twenty-one and he was twenty-three. They had never been to a Halloween party "because it seemed stupid and superficial." But it was a "kind, distinguished man" who convinced them in an entirely unexpected manner. They met him almost every morning in a coffee bar where they would have breakfast. During months of casual conversation, the man won the trust of the couple. When he invited them to a Halloween party, they decided to go. The address led them to a house out in the country. They were well received, although it all seemed to them "a bit ridiculous." There were about fifty people invited, all dressed as witches, vampires, and zombies. The only illumination was given by a few candles. The couple were the only ones without costumes and with their faces not covered. They did not yet know it, but they had been chosen as sacrificial victims of a Black Mass.

They felt uncomfortable and wanted to leave, but they were already there and so tried to fit in with the scene. They ate and drank. They were offered some drinks "by the distinguished man at the bar." At one point, they were negatively struck by the sudden appearance of a man dressed in black, "with a large cape and a hood hiding his face. Everyone except the two of them got down on their knees. . . . He placed his hands on each of them in turn as they began speaking in an incomprehensible language." Without any previous knowledge of the occult world and considering such things "just fantasy and make believe," they thought they were watching "some sort of game for the feast of Halloween." This time, however, the desire to leave grew urgent. They both had a headache and felt weak. They went for the door but found it locked. They lost consciousness.

To their good fortune, they were still alive when morning came. The young man was the first to awake. Next to him, his girlfriend was completely naked. All over her body were cuts, scratches, bruises, and various signs of abuse. The large house was empty. At the hospital, they discovered she had been raped and that there was ketamine in their blood. Several days later, he returned to the house in the country. The owner made it clear that, unless they wanted trouble, nothing ever happened: "that evening never existed."

Over the following days, the girl was persecuted by anonymous phone calls. Terrorized, she did not leave home. Naturally, "the distinguished man" disappeared from the scene. They moved to a different city and eventually got married. They met a journalist who guaranteed their anonymity, and explained how they decided to tell their story because it must "be made known, especially to youth who think that this holiday is something really great and cool, but that during the feast of Halloween horrible things take place. Kids should be warned for sure; they must not fear going against the grain. . . . My life," the girl emphasized, "was ruined, and I bear the signs of those ruins in my soul and in my mind." Concerning the "horrible things," for the sake of offering a further example, we should not forget that from the first phases of the investigation into the homicide of an English university student in Perugia that happened on the evening of November 1, the authorities judged not improbable a relation with the setting and the orgiastic rites of Halloween.

The Joy of All Saints

The aforementioned events demonstrate how around this presumed holiday for children celebrated on the eve of All Saints' Day, there is a shady commercialization of evil, through masks, subliminal messages, and advertising in the media.

Significantly, after a period of culpable indifference, the Church, including the highest levels of the hierarchy, has begun to sound the alarm with insistence. This alarm, however, has gone unheeded, and in some ways has not been understood by the majority of Catholics, now inured by the dominant culture. The Vatican secretary of state, Cardinal Tarcisio Bertone, commenting on the decision of the court of Strasbourg that had prohibited placing the cross in classrooms, observed that "unfortunately, this Europe of the third millennium leaves us only the pumpkins of the feast on the eve of November 1, and takes from us our dearest symbols."

Bitter words that fit well with the many severe condemnations of Halloween that, year after year, appear among Catholics. But also on the rise are the communities, parish groups, and dioceses around the world that organize parties and catechesis groups to promote the authentic sense of the communion of saints and the reverence of the faithful departed. The John XXIII Community, along with the dioceses of Massa Carrara and La Spezia, for example, organize alternative gatherings to counter what has been termed "a great satanic rite." Initiatives like these are held in countries with a strong Catholic tradition such as France, Spain, and Chile. Members of the

Spanish Episcopal Conference caution that the feast of Halloween "has a background in the occult and is absolutely anti-Christian," and therefore exhort families to "direct the celebration toward the good and the beautiful rather than toward terror, fear, and death." In light of this, prayer vigils and recreational and educational events are organized in many Spanish cities, including Madrid.

In Paris, experiments are being made with alternative parties for youth and children, during which amusement is not separated from the witness of faith and the affirmation of Christian hope in the face of death. Along these same lines is an initiative promoted in Santiago de Chile, with children and adolescents who celebrate wearing costumes of angels, princes and princesses, and the saints. Such costumes are connected to positive themes to transform death and darkness into light and life, terror into joy, violence and fear into hope and peace. The same logic has been implemented in Italy through the Sentinels of the Dawn project in many cities, distributing on the eve of All Saints' Day in the streets, on the doors of churches, and in car windows brochures and images of the saints. The initiative is called "Holyween." The initiator of the idea was Fr. Andrea Brugnoli, who explained his desire to "fill the cities not with monsters but with beautiful faces, with invitations to reflect how sanctity is possible even today in concrete lives." Smiles, serenity, and joy come from goodness, not the dark and disturbing faces of malice hung in shops, which, as in the case of the couple in the story above, turned out to be authentic antechambers of Hell.

The feast of Halloween is a Hosannah to the devil, who, once adored, even for just a night, thinks he can boast of rights over a person. If we do not realize this, we should not be surprised at children who cannot get to sleep, agitated and rowdy or depressed youth, obsessed and potentially suicidal. *In fact, Halloween is a sort of spiritualistic session, almost always presented as an innocent game. Through fun and games, children are educated in the tricks of evil, without realizing they are dealing with very serious matters. It is the continuation of the deceit of the devil that makes many sins seem no longer to be considered as such. Everything is camouflaged in the form of needs, freedom, or personal pleasure.* Man himself is the arbiter of what is or is not sinful. *In this way, man is transformed into his own god, and this is exactly what the devil wants, from the very beginning. Just consider the temptation in the Garden of Eden: "For God knows that when you eat of it your eyes will be opened, and you will be like God, knowing good and evil"* (Gen. 3:5).

One must not forget that Halloween is superimposed on a Christian feast of extraordinary spiritual value, which celebrates the communion of saints through which we commemorate our beloved deceased and pray for them in the vision and certainty of eternal life. As Vatican II teaches in *Lumen Gentium* (49), by means of prayer, the union "of the wayfarers with the brethren who have gone to sleep in the peace of Christ is not in the least weakened or interrupted … [but] is strengthened by communication of spiritual goods." The spiritual flow of prayer creates continuity between Heaven and earth in a common vision of light and hope that, as St. Paul says, "does not disappoint" (Rom. 5:5). "For this is the will of my Father, that everyone who sees the Son and believes in him should have eternal life; and I will raise him up at the last day" (John 6:40). In reality, this is the exact opposite of what is being transmitted with Halloween, where death is portrayed in its most devastating form in a lie without happiness and without hope, alongside increasingly frequent satanic symbolism and the evocation of the so-called living dead.

Paradise Conquered

The devil tries to take us to his kingdom with all the means he has at his disposal and which, of course, are always contrary to Christian morality. He does everything in his power to get man to lose his soul through continually proposing temptations and seductions. He uses cunning of every type, but his game is always out in the open: instead of life he proposes death; instead of joy, desperation; instead of good, evil; love, hate; purity, perversity; Paradise, Hell.

The Kingdom of God is Paradise. The aim of every man's life is to merit it. The path indicated to us is that of Jesus: "I am the living bread which came down from heaven; if anyone eats of this bread, he will live forever" (John 6:51). It does not matter what life he leads, if he is rich or poor, alone or accompanied, healthy or sick. What counts is eternal life, to save one's soul.

This is not an easy path. *The road to Paradise always passes through Calvary*. The Christian, as opposed to those of other religions, knows this with absolute certainty. In one of his most well-known expressions, Mahatma Ghandi stated that "he who walks the path of truth shall not stumble." We can say with certainty that this is an absolute falsity, as fascinating as it is deceptive. If it is true that the path of truth is the upright path, it is also true that it is uphill and full of stumbling blocks. This does not mean that it is not a joyful path.

The path Jesus proposes is demanding. It is not something for relativists or for the tolerant who say one direction is as good as another. "I have not come to bring peace, but a sword" (Matt. 10:34). To be a Christian means to be on Jesus' side. "He who does not take up his cross and follow me is not worthy of me" (Matt. 10:38). At the same time, the Christian knows how to be, like Jesus, tough with evil but tender with those in need.

Every victory is the fruit of a sacrifice proportionate to that which must be attained. In this, we enjoy the promise that no one will remain disappointed. *In light of this we can understand the need to mistrust those who propose shortcuts, the easy road, easy riches and success. One encounters diabolical snares at every turn in the road, the typical deception of magicians and witches.*

A powder in exchange for love, attending a rite in exchange for that thing I so long for; wearing a charm, a ring, a bracelet, avoiding the path of a black cat or not walking under a ladder to be protected from adverse events. Even if these are apparently innocent or naïve superstitions, one must always beware because God is not in them. *And one of the terrible realities of the devil is that when one is truly involved with him, he grants what he promises. Never, however, does what he grants, no matter how extraordinary and amazing, produce joy or lead to happiness. Just as he promised Jesus in the desert, the devil can give wealth and power, but above all he procures great sadness. In fact, in all my long experience and that of my exorcist colleagues, we have seen that the devil has never been able to transmit serenity to the men or women who entrust themselves to him, despite whatever riches or power or pleasures he might bestow upon them. They leave behind them a trail of pain, death, dejection, and sorrow. One might even say that this is his signature: unhappiness is the mark of the devil.*

All of us have experienced crosses we must bear in life. If we endure them by offering them to the Lord, those crosses have great value and become a "light yoke," leaving behind a trail of serenity and concord leading to Heaven. When one experiences the value of suffering, suffering becomes a cause of joy. *I have met people with grave illnesses who were happy and who would not have exchanged their condition for healing. If, on the other hand, one lives the cross with anger, it becomes much heavier. If it becomes a cause for rebellion against God, it can transform into a cause of damnation. At any rate, if one does not give to suffering a good motivation, it is absurd to put up with it, because we were created for joy, not for suffering. St. Augustine said, "Lord, You have created us for Yourself and our heart is restless until it rests in You." Far from Jesus Christ, we cannot emerge victorious from this difficult battle. Enmity, depression, unhappiness, family strife — which ever more frequently produce unbridgeable hatreds and even homicide and suicide, not to mention euthanasia and abortion — are all concrete examples of defeat at the hands of evil. And when it is a matter of those things closely tied to choices between life and death, the devil displays all his ability.*

The Passion is necessary for the Resurrection, therefore. *And the Resurrection brought with it three fundamental fruits for man: it defeated death; it overcame the corruption of the body; it opened the gates of Paradise, doors that were closed by the angels at the moment when Adam and Eve were chased out of Eden. Concerning Paradise, St. Paul highlights, "What no eye has seen, nor ear heard, nor the heart of man conceived, what God has prepared for those who love him" (1 Cor. 2:9). In essence, death is no longer a definitive evil, our body will rise glorious like the body of Christ, and we shall see God face-to-face, we shall live with Him in Heaven.*

These are three fruits to take into serious consideration every time we find ourselves in the face of suffering, a cross too difficult to carry. One can certainly say that Jesus as man, in the most difficult moment He lived in the Garden of Gethsemane, had the strength to accept the Passion thanks to the prospect of the joy of the Resurrection.

The House of Deep Hatred

It is not God who sends us to Hell; we run there on our own legs. The mercy of God is infinite. He is always ready to welcome us with open arms, to the final moment of our lives. Sr. Faustina Kowalska, the saint who received in a vision the image of the Divine Mercy, was told dozens of times by Jesus to make known to men how great His love is for them, and His ability to forgive and to welcome them, as long as they desire it. The problem, added Jesus to Sr. Faustina in one of her visions, is that they do not want it: "My daughter, look upon My merciful heart. The flames of mercy burn Me: I want to pour it out upon souls, but they do not want to believe in My goodness." In another passage, Jesus reminds her that "when a soul exalts My goodness, Satan trembles and flees to the depths of Hell." In the face of Jesus, the devil is afraid, because all his inferiority is laid bare, all his weakness as a creature is made apparent before his Creator, of which he is fully aware.

Sr. Faustina explains in her diary, which she wrote following the mystical dialogues she had with the Lord, that Jesus suffers terribly because of our sin and rejoices like the father of the prodigal son when sinners entrust themselves to Him, even if only at the moment of death. "I myself will defend at the moment of their death those who proclaim My great Mercy. Even if their sins were black like the night, when a sinner turns to My Mercy, he renders Me the greatest glory and is the pride of My passion."

The servant of God Fr. Giovanni Semeria, who was not a mystic (although a great man of faith, charity, and prayer), explained to his audience at the end of the nineteenth century his hope in the merciful God: "God is love: *Deus Caritas est.* God loves man and this must be said with great passion. He loves us and begs for our love. He loves us and at the final moment of His life repeats this one last time. He, this rejected lover, comes to us to hear a word of repentance, to expiate a life of rebuffs."

As recited in the Second Eucharistic Prayer, in the original complete text of the *Canon of Hippolytus,* Christ immolated Himself "to defeat the power of death, to break the bonds of the devil, to crush Hell, to bring light to the just, to put an end to their imprisonment, and to announce to them the Resurrection."

To the very end, Jesus labored to steal from the sad destiny of Hell those who refuse Him, the destiny into which the devil tries to drag them to the very last. In this way, St. Faustina, in the moment in which she became aware of the enormous difficulty to be overcome in carrying out the work that Jesus entrusted her, pointed out: "Now I understood that Satan hates Mercy more than ever. It is his greatest torment." Then, with renewed hope, she added, "But the word of the Lord will be fulfilled. The word of God is alive and the difficulties will not annihilate the work of God, but demonstrate that they are of God."

These concepts have been repeated hundreds of times in the apparitions of Medjugorje, where the Virgin Mary often asks us to "pray for those who are under the power of Satan," because "Satan is strong and is always waiting in ambush and wants to destroy not only human life but also nature and the planet you live on." Always during her apparitions, Mary invites us to place our confidence in prayer and humble surrender to Divine Mercy. Interesting in this respect are the two apparitions in 1830 in the church at Rue du Bac in Paris, in which she not only entrusted to the visionaries the image of the so-called Miraculous Medal, but also invited them to come "to the foot of this altar. Here graces will be poured out on all, especially the people who ask for them with fervor, on the little and the great. . . . I will be with you."

God wants all of us in Heaven. He gives us the instruments to get there, and even offers Himself and His Mother. So why does Hell exist, who created it?

It was certainly not God. The demons emphasize this proudly during the exorcisms. Fr. Candido once found himself with a demon that did not want to leave a person. "Leave this body," he told it, "go back to Hell. God prepared a nice hot home for you."

The demon's response was unsettling: "You don't understand a thing, you know nothing. He did not create Hell. He did not even think of it. We demons created it."

The devil created Hell from nothing. At any rate, Hell might not even be a place. Some theologians have spoken of a non-place, based on the concept that Hell is the negation of God. According to the facts, therefore, it is practically impossible to define it. Many saints have had visions of Hell, but they are always different and always in function of their intellectual and cognitive abilities.

The *Catechism of the Catholic Church,* in point 212 of the *Compendium,* recalls that Hell "consists in the eternal damnation of those who die in mortal sin through their own free choice. The principal suffering of Hell is eternal separation from God in whom alone we can have the life and happiness for which we were created and for which we long." Reference is then made to the words of Jesus in Matthew 25:41: "Depart from me, you cursed, into eternal fire." Immediately following this, in point 213, the *Catechism* explains that God wants "all to come to repentance." Nevertheless, having created man completely free and responsible, He respects our will. "Therefore, it is the human person who freely excludes himself from communion with God if at the moment of death he persists in mortal sin and refuses the merciful love of God."

What we know with certainty, therefore, is that Hell is populated by those who refuse, or better, who reject in every way the love of God and his omnipotence. This was one of the questions the visionary Mirjana of Medjugorje asked Our Lady, concerned with the possibility that the damned could change their minds: "But if one of the damned were to repent, could Jesus take him from Hell into Paradise?" Our Lady answered, almost despondently: "He could, but they do not want to."

They do not want to because their choice was made voluntarily without return. Such words recall the Gospel parable of the rich man "who was clothed in purple and fine linen and who feasted sumptuously every day," who, upon dying and going to Hell, wanted Lazarus, who had also died but was in "Abraham's bosom," to go to his brothers and warn them that if they do not lead an upright life they are destined to suffer for eternity. It does not say that he repented of how he conducted his own life; he does not ask how he can get out of the situation he finds himself in, but would like Lazarus to come down with a bit of water or, at least, to go and warn those of his house that they might not end up in the same place. Here too, the answer leaves us amazed: "They have Moses and the prophets. … If they do not hear Moses and the prophets, neither will they be convinced if someone should rise from the dead."

This is a concept that Dante expressed through the mouth of Beatrice, with the two famous tercets in the fifth canto of the *Paradiso*:

> Christians, be ye more serious in your movements;
> Be ye not like a feather at each wind,
> And think not every water washes you.
> Ye have the Old and the New Testament,
> And the Pastor of the Church who guideth you
> Let this suffice you unto your salvation.

The problem is that those who seek their own damnation and stubbornly follow this end become in all ways like Satan. Ever more perverse, but also prouder and more convinced that his choice is the right one, the one capable of fulfilling his freedom and his feeling of omnipotence. And the height of perversity accompanies the height of deception. The one who lives in sin is in himself so perverse that, in the same manner as the devil, he deceives himself. Be careful, however, not to think that grave sin is something committed by the few and is just an impulsive action. In a society like ours, one often lives in a sort of desensitization to sin.

What is sinful is no longer identified as such. And thus, sin is added upon sin. Thousands of occasions offer plausible excuses for our failings. One becomes increasingly dissolute without even realizing it. "Grave sin," noticed Semeria, in a passage of a famous Lenten sermon that remained etched in the memory of Benedict XV, "is not and cannot be an extemporized phenomenon. One does not become bad in a day. Just as one climbs the mountain of the virtues slowly, by little steps, so too does one descend slowly the slippery slope of vice, by little steps." Warning in this way the people packed into the Roman Basilica of St. Lawrence in Damaso, among whom were high-ranking clergy, Queen Margherita of Savoy with her retinue, magistrates, and famous professors with Masonic leanings, he invited all to exercise the nearly obsolete practice of the examination of conscience: "My brothers, you who, through a correct fear of Hell, seek to persuade yourselves that it does not exist, be honest and tell me how many times and in how many ways God has called you and you have refused the invitations?"

Many saints, for example St. Teresa of Ávila, have had terrible visions of Hell populated by a multitude of souls, while others continued to fall in throngs. The description given by St. Veronica Giuliani is meticulous. Lucifer, in the center, controls everything with his eyes. Immediately under him is Judas. Then the clergy divided according to category, in rigorous order of importance. Last, the immense crowd of the damned. And naturally, as in Paradise, not all are the same. Dante put so much emphasis on this latter concept through his hypothesis of the fitting punishment — in other words, the close correlation between the type of sin committed in life and the punishment suffered in Hell. The great interest in Veronica Giuliani's vision was due to the miraculous discovery of her writings in twenty-two thousand pages by an eighty-year-old French pilgrim long after her death. Before that discovery, no one had thought the woman was a saint. She lived and had her mystical visions and wrote of them in complete hiddenness.

The Occult, Spiritualism, and Magic

"When you come into the land which the Lord your God gives you, you shall not learn to follow the abominable practices of those nations. There shall not be found among you anyone who burns his son or his daughter as an offering, anyone who practices divination, a soothsayer, or an augur, or a sorcerer, or a charmer, or a medium, or a wizard, or a necromancer. For whoever does these things is an abomination to the Lord" (Deut. 18:9–12). *Throughout all history, Israel has always been given the alternative: either be faithful to the one true God or fall into idolatry. This situation is analogous to what has always happened throughout the history of Christianity and which happens still today: abandon God and give oneself over to idols, in the ways proper to each historical period, although the idols are always the same.*

It is said that in Italy there are twelve million people who have had some form of contact with magicians and fortune tellers or who frequent them regularly. A very high number, to be linked with the ever-lower turnout for Sunday Mass, the sacraments, and the celebrations for the important feasts. It would be even higher if one were to add to that number the host of those who assiduously read their horoscope.

The signs of the Zodiac are often dismissed as mere entertainment. There are, however, many people who truly believe in the affinities dictated by the stars. The question among acquaintances, "What is your sign?" is quite frequent and when one hears it asked, one often perceives a chilling spiritual void. Television, as always in these cases, is a formidable manipulator and justifies itself by saying that it is only entertainment. But how can one consider it a mere amusement if those who create the horoscopes, besides their considerable profits, are able to tell us in detail all the things that will happen to us that day, or week or month and even year, starting with the most intimate personal experiences? Ours and other people's private lives and sentiments are things which everyone takes most seriously. One who thinks he can influence them, and does so as a game because he is convinced he knows how it is done or for mere profit, is at any rate a deceiver. Often, the authors and editors of the newspapers and mass media where these horoscopes are found circumvent the accusation of dabbling in superstition, maintaining that they propose these things to give people a glimmer of hope, tested as they are by the hardships of life. But hope, when founded on nothing, is only deception.

These idols disorient, distract, and distance from the true motive of happiness which is in Jesus Christ. The list is quite long and each of us knows perfectly well what composes it. *All these idols are the fruit of the conviction of being able to do without God. One no longer wants to believe in an invisible world presented to us by revelation: God, angels and demons, Heaven, Hell and Purgatory, the immortality of the soul, and the Last Judgment. The paradox is that one ends up believing in a parallel world made up of cosmic forces and entities, of fantasy personalities who act mysteriously, outside the pale of normal sensibilities, whom one can approach and understand only through the teachings of occultists, spiritualists, gurus, and so-called experts of various pseudo-sciences. They are people who use these powers to read thoughts and the future, materialize objects, and influence nature and other people for better or worse. They are people with the ability to enter into direct contact with spirits, with the dead, and even with extraterrestrial beings.*

And in this way, instead of turning to a priest, one seeks the intervention of a wizard, follows the counsel of magicians and spiritists, and entrusts oneself to gurus. Instead of following the practice of the sacraments and prayer, one carries out strange rites, pronouncing unknown formulas, speaking with spirits. Instead of placing one's hope in the immortality of the soul, in resurrection and in the return of Christ at the end of time, one scrutinizes the heavens awaiting a UFO, or the arrival of extraterrestrials, hoping in mysterious entities who will come and save the world, believing in millenarian mythologies that can do nothing but plunge one into desperation. Instead of entrusting one's protection to Christ crucified, to Our Lady, to the saints and one's guardian angel, one fills one's house, office, and car with amulets, horns, horseshoes, and crooked nails.

The God who is too "medieval" to be appropriate for the times and who scandalizes the knowledge of modernity is unfortunately substituted with superstitions of the most varied forms and diabolical perversions. The alleged modernity of such things consists only in the way they are publicized: through television, e-mail, social media, forums, and websites. *Where there is no faith, where the certain knowledge of revelation is substituted by mystification, it is easy for every sort of invention to arise, especially fantastical constructs made by man. For those anchored in the Word of God, all that is not God's Word is merely human. And when man does not follow God, he ends up aligning himself with the devil.*

Spiritualism and the occult are a clear proof of this. *Such things open doors to the devil. Evoking the dead to have an answer to some question of ours is a common practice. There are many who speak of this as a positive thing, that can even serve to heal the emotional wounds left by the death of someone dear. Every now and then, even on TV, one hears talk of mothers who say they have rediscovered their ability to trust after being able, thanks to spiritualism, to get into contact with their prematurely deceased child, quite often due to car accidents.*

In reality, they are asking for answers from the dead which the Christian faith has already fully given. We do not consider the latter more convincing, unfortunately, because we have met priests and religious who do not convince us. We are desperate, vulnerable to temptations, and we surrender ourselves to whomever. Many young people try spiritualism out of curiosity. Spiritualism is practiced in many ways: there is the Ouija board, the cup game, the table game. It is practiced with the magnetic recorder, with the supposed automatic transcriber. There are schools of spiritism like the Movement of Hope, which, dramatically, boasts of having a few priests among its members.

And none of this is new. These paths have been trod from the dawn of time. In the fifteenth century, an innocent philosopher like Marsilio Ficino, one of the minds behind Renaissance thought who was formed in the Medici circle of Florence, wrote: "Man stands in God's stead, who lives in all the elements, who takes care of all and, present on earth, is not absent from the heavens. And not only does he make use of the elements but also of all the beings that live in the elements: terrestrial, aquatic, and winged to use as food, for his comfort, for his pleasure; of the higher, celestial beings for magical doctrine and for their miracles.... And not only does man dominate the animals with cruelty, but he also governs them, assists them, trains them. His is the universal Providence of God, who is universal cause. Man, therefore, who provides universally, both for living beings as for inanimate beings, is in a certain sense a god."

Analogously, Giovanni Pico della Mirandola, Ficino's student, a believer and a cabalist, a cultivator of what, at the time, was called the magical sciences, portrays God speaking words directed to Adam and thus to all humanity: "I made you neither celestial nor terrestrial, neither mortal nor immortal, because you, as if on your own, were the free and sovereign creator, formed by your own doing according to your preferred form. You can degenerate, lowering yourself to the inferior beings, the brutes or, following the impulse of your spirit, regenerate and elevate yourself to the greater spirits, the divine."

Therefore, after having explained that in the celestial beings God placed one type of seed and in the brutes another type, clearly differentiated in their actions, placing them in opposition, Pico della Mirandola emphasizes that God placed in man "the seed of every species and the germ of all life: according to how each one shall cultivate them, they will develop and produce in him their fruits."

From the theological point of view, one could say these statements straddle the line between sound and unsound. The essence of things is quite clear to both. The essence of God and of human beings in God's image and likeness is fully illuminated—just as it was during the Renaissance, where the particular dedication to beauty in all the arts was sought in the attempt to reflect the greatness and beauty of God. One finds a demonstration of this in Michelangelo's sonnets. At the same time, both in Ficino and in Pico della Mirandola, there is the lucid awareness of the fact that man can directly interfere with the "superior beings," can manipulate the mysterious forces of spiritism and magic. Naturally, it is the way man approaches these things that makes the difference. One can ascend to God with humility or with the diabolical pride of one seeking to take His place.

We know for sure that Ficino chose to become a priest in his old age, while Pico della Mirandola remained on the borderline of heresy. Neither of them attained the heights of faith that two of their contemporaries and common friends reached: Girolamo Savonarola and Michelangelo Buonarroti. These two were tormented by the experience of evil, blinded by the light of Christ (characterized, though in different ways, by an imposing effort of interior moralizing), and certain they could ascend to the divine vision and perfection only by surrendering themselves to God Himself. They were fully aware of the warning in Deuteronomy that those who practice magic and invoke the dead are an abomination to God. Those were particularly difficult years for the true Faith, in some ways quite similar to ours. The Council of Trent, although moving within a Counter-Reformation logic, was forced to come to terms with the need to draw the line in the figurative arts and music between sacred and profane, divine and diabolical. At a certain point, the elimination of music from the liturgy was even contemplated. It was said that the cardinals changed their minds, however, after having listened to Palestrina's *Missa Papae Marcelli*, in honor of the deceased Pope Marcello II.

At the end of the Christian's path, however tortuous and complicated, truth always emerges in all its splendor. The discrimination between good and evil follows the very same logic that distinguishes the beautiful from the ugly, the sublime from the horrid.

Satanic Cults

Satanism, in all its aspects, is the form of the occult par excellence. A life of grave sin accompanied by progressive habituation to evil can lead a person to make culpable choices in favor of the devil, at times without even realizing the gravity and ineluctability of what he is doing. Frequent blasphemies, when they are not merely a filler curse word but a conscious gesture, express hatred for God and proximity to the devil. Spiritualist sessions are often carried out with direct contact. The client believes he is speaking with his beloved departed, but he is really communicating with the devil. The constant frequenting of certain nightclubs often leads down a path to perdition, in which the usual things are present: alcohol, drugs, sex, satanic cults. One can of course enter a cult through friends, just as one can be drawn into such settings through a predilection for perversion, or through a passion for a certain type of music and so forth.

Belonging to a satanic cult is relatively simple. Instructions can even be found on the Internet. Getting out of one can be quite difficult, if not nearly impossible. They are usually very small groups because they can meet more easily to perform their rites, and it is easier to keep the various members under control and act without being detected. Satanic rock music, especially among young people, is often used as a common bond. They gather for this type of music, they frequent each other through it, and they begin to think in terms of satanic projects inspired by it. They strengthen their bond of complicity through the use of drugs that this type of music spreads and exalts.

Satanic rock also promotes forms of solitary satanism, or as a couple. It teaches an unrestrained individualism, absolute nihilism, and combats every type of social order, most especially the family and the Catholic Faith. Forms of solitary satanism, promoted on the Internet or, in some settings, through the distribution of pamphlets, is expressed as a true pedagogy of suicide. I once had to sequester from an adolescent a booklet that taught a consecration to Satan as well showing various ways to kill oneself. Considering the growth throughout the world of suicides among adolescents, one wonders if this is one of the reasons.

Satanic cults constitute the highest degree of consecration to the works of the devil, with all the terrible actions they bring: from the profanation of bodies (we have seen how sex is the most common key to access these settings), to the profanation of the sacred carried out in all its forms (there are priests who perform Black Masses during which they profane the Body and Blood of Christ), to human sacrifice carried out within the context of satanic rites as a sign of total belonging to the world of Satan.

There is no lack of saints who, when attending Mass, and in particular at the moment of Consecration, had the clear perception of the impurity (or purity) of the priest. Faustina Kowalska tells in her diary that while attending Mass celebrated by her confessor, she saw the Child Jesus on the altar smiling to all and made it clear he was quite fond of the soul of the celebrating priest. On the contrary, there is the case of Teresa of Ávila, who at one point in her life, ill and tired, had to attend a Mass celebrated by a priest toward whom she felt a certain horror, because she perceived in a clear manner all the gravity of his sin. At the moment of the elevation, she saw the luminous host held by hands become as black as coal. This showed to her the fact that the transformation of the bread and wine into the Body and Blood of Christ takes place nevertheless, even when the priest is animated by evil.

From this point of view, one can certainly say that satanists firmly believe in the real presence of Jesus in the Eucharist—paradoxically, much more than many Catholics. Many thefts of consecrated hosts happen for this reason, and, unfortunately, there is no lack of priests perverted by the devil who belong to satanic sects. And there always have been. I am often asked why a priest falls so low. What can be said is that the abyss of perversity is unfathomable and that the devil always grants what he promises — in exchange for one's soul, of course.

This is the concept of selling one's soul to the devil, which in literature became famous in the character of Faust, but other examples come to mind as well. For example: Oscar Wilde's *The Picture of Dorian Gray*, or Bulgakov's *The Master and Margarita*. One can sell one's soul even to the perverse and egocentric mirage of overcoming all limits, without changing the results in terms of perdition and destruction, like Captain Ahab in *Moby-Dick*. So too can one construct one's entire life and fortune on a clever deceit and discover in the end that the same ability with which we have deceived others has cast us into the void, like the protagonist of Gorgol's *Dead Souls*.

Even more so in Gogol, the fascinating story "The Portrait" in *Petersburg Tales* ought to be analyzed. In this work he expressed all the ways by which the devil acts upon the human race, even the most apparently improbable, and their consequences. The same art, in all its possible expressions, can never, by its very nature, avoid aligning with either good or evil, and thus renders obvious both choices perhaps more than any other realization of human genius. At the same time, Gogol's narrative illustrates the only possible route of redemption: total dedication to God. Through this, the artistic form acquires that extraordinary capacity to transmit the divine which is proper to the beautiful.

The powerful discourse of Benedict XVI comes to mind, given to the city of Rome on the occasion of the feast of the Immaculate Conception in 2009: "Every day, in fact, in the newspapers, on television, and on the radio, bad news is broadcast, repeated, amplified, so that we become used to the most terrible things and inured to them, and in a certain way poisoned, since the negative effect is never completely eliminated but accumulates day after day. The heart hardens and thoughts grow gloomy. For this reason, the city needs Mary, whose presence speaks of God, reminds us of the victory of Grace over sin, and leads us to hope, even in the most difficult human situations. … The border between good and evil runs through every heart and none of us should feel entitled to judge others. Rather, each one must feel duty bound to improve him or herself." The mass media, the pope continues, "always tends to make us feel like 'spectators,' as if evil concerned only others and certain things could never happen to us. Instead, we are all 'actors' and, for better or for worse, our behavior has an influence on others. We often complain of the pollution of the atmosphere. … Yet, there is another kind of contamination, less perceptible to the senses, but equally dangerous. It is the pollution of the spirit; it makes us smile less, makes our faces gloomier, less likely to greet each other or look each other in the eye. … People become bodies and these bodies lose their soul, they become things, faceless objects that can be exchanged and consumed."

This, then, is the diabolical game, reintroduced by culture, by habits, by some forms of art, and by most of the media, to which we always risk becoming habituated. I sell my soul, I buy yours, or I act as if neither ever existed — at times simply because I want to, at times because I have adapted myself to a certain level of superficiality, if not an outright absence of human relationships, that I am no longer capable of realizing. And who cares, anyway. Exactly this happens to the young Raskolnikov, the protagonist in Dostoevsky's *Crime and Punishment* who, without even realizing it, develops within himself the conditions that lead him to commit the double homicide that marks his life, carried out as if they were unavoidable, according to the inner logic of things, because others like him had considered the matter exactly as he did. "Later," the novel reads, "he could not understand where he had attained so much cunning, so much that his mind, occasionally, went blank, and he no longer had perception of his body." Only afterward, "a dark sensation of distressing solitude, of irrelevance, was revealed to his soul. . . . This was the most tormenting sensation of all he had ever felt in his life."

This is the cunning of the devil that draws great profit from a society that not only denies his existence, but also the existence of the soul. If I refuse to believe in the devil, it is easier for him to act; if I refuse to believe in the existence of my soul or act as if it did not exist, it no longer matters if I put it at risk or lose it.

One sells one's soul, and loses it, and then it becomes much more difficult to regain possession of it, if one does eventually realize one's mistake and wants to turn back. Not unlike that character of Guareschi, a lifelong communist, as hardened as he is ingenuous, who proclaims he is an anticlerical atheist, who naturally does not believe in the existence of the soul. When an old man of faith, considered to be a classic example of religious bigotry, offers to buy his soul for a modest though not negligible sum of money, he decides to take the offer, thinking he would be giving him nothing in exchange for the money. A while later, after a number of vicissitudes in life, feeling his emptiness within, he considers the soul he has sold and asks for it back. But the astute old man wants his money back too, because that man has finally understood the value of his soul.

The formula for membership in satanic cults is a sort of sale of one's soul to the devil. *I have burned many such formulas of consecration to Satan. They all express more or less the same concepts: "Satan you are my god, I want to belong only to you, but give me in exchange riches, pleasure, health, success." All things that have to do with this world. The so-called pleasures of the flesh. The entire kingdom of Satan, at any rate, is based on this world. In the other world there is only infernal darkness.*

When Satan tempts Jesus, he essentially states, "all the kingdoms of the earth are mine and I can give them to whomever I want." Jesus does not respond by telling him this is a lie, but rather: "It is written: you shall not worship other gods, but only the Lord your God."

What I know about satanic cults has been told to me by people who with great difficulty and serious risk have decided to leave them. They come out scarred and with diabolical influences that provoke great suffering in them. To be liberated from them they need exorcisms. Quite often they live in a state of terror. They are threatened. They realize they can be murdered at any moment. There are many stories in the news, in Italy and abroad, that document how murderers are trained in these environments. In the United States it is almost systematic that those who try to leave them are killed. In Italy, it happens more rarely. The terror these people feel comes from the direct experience of the consequences of curses, and the satanic cults perform curses against those who choose to leave. The news is full of stories of suicides and mysterious automobile accidents.

I have been involved in two cases of this type, very serious, for several years now. The first concerns a man who was a victim of a satanic cult that continues to curse him and his family. Over these four years I have succeeded in liberating his wife and children. With him, I have reached the point where the devil no longer yells every time he says he wants him dead. The devil now knows he must go, but he still resists. This family knows exactly who put the curse on them, and they know who belongs to the cult. Such information can be found by interrogating the demon. In this case, the demon himself confirmed the names of the members. And it happened that when one of the members died, the demon said during the exorcism that he no longer belonged to the cult.

The second case involves a girl in Northern Italy who was the victim of a very strong curse by a satanic group formed by cloistered nuns. A terrible thing, difficult to comprehend and to believe due to the context in which it formed, unfortunately; but history provides other examples of consecrated religious who have dedicated themselves to Satan. And when this happens, the evil that is unleashed is enormous. The girl frequented these sisters, as do many other normal people. She helped them, at times even providing for their needs by donating money.

But how can we say it was them?

She was the one who understood this. She came to that realization. There are many who are able to understand precisely who it was who cursed them. A friend of mine, an exorcist bishop, performed many exorcisms on her. He asked for my help because the curse that struck her was tremendous. This woman is a high-level musician and can no longer perform in concerts because the devil blocks her hands. It happens suddenly, in the middle of concerts, for no reason. During the exorcisms she has no reaction. A very difficult thing to understand. We have not been able to initiate a dialogue with the demon in her, as happens in other cases of possession. After the exorcism, she is ill for several days, and then seems healed for a week. And then it starts all over again. In her profession, she needs to practice at least four hours a day. After the exorcism she can for a time. But not concerts. There are many exorcists who have performed exorcisms on her, but unfortunately with the same results.

The Essence of Sin

I SUFFER WHEN WE *are not able to liberate a person from these terrible situations of diabolic influence. I suffer because I feel how much they need it. I understand we are limited, that our faith is insufficient. At times, I even feel a bit of envy toward the apostles who expelled demons in just one encounter. Many saints reached that level of union with Christ that they could liberate someone from the devil even by their presence.* Don Bosco, when he was very old and was almost incapable of moving from his room to the chapel, had reached such a level of sanctity and ability as an exorcist that the devil could not even bear his presence. There is the story of a French girl, demon possessed, who after years of wandering from one exorcist to another decided to visit Don Bosco. She went to the chapel where the saint usually celebrated Mass in the hope of finding him. The moment she entered the church where Don Bosco was at the altar, the demon fled and the girl was liberated. St. Catherine of Siena also cast out demons with great efficacy through her prayers.

It is a question of faith, great faith. And when this is lacking or one feels one has little, we must ask for it with insistence. Once again, Benedict XVI's above-mentioned discourse for the Immaculate Conception can help us: "What does Mary tell the city? Of what does her presence remind us? It reminds us that 'where sin increased, grace abounded all the more' (Rom. 5:20), as the Apostle Paul wrote. She is the Immaculate Mother who tells people in our day too: Do not be afraid, Jesus has defeated evil, He has uprooted it, delivering us from its rule."

The entire Bible tells us that, in the face of man's continual infidelity, God is patient, patient, patient. Then, at a certain point, punishment arrives. But it is not God who punishes, but man who punishes himself, or who punish one another. It must be clear: it is not God who sends punishments. Men who pursue the paths of malice transform everything into evil, and evil never builds, it always separates and destroys. St. Augustine said that if God did not keep them under control, "demons would kill everyone." And there are many, many demons. A demon once said to me, "If we were visible, we would block out the sun."

The angels, however, are immensely more numerous. And we must not be afraid of the devil, because as we have just read, Jesus has defeated evil from the root, liberating us from its dominion. We ought to be afraid of sin, however. In this regard, Paul VI held that "everything that defends us from sin defends us from the evil one."

St. John of the Cross, in one of his lesser works titled *Cautions,* addressing his Discalced Carmelites, teaches to take "as an example the wife of Lot (Gen. 19:26) who was transformed into a salt column because in her concern she turned to look at the ruins of the inhabitants of the city of Sodom. This happened that you might understand what is the will of God: even if you lived among demons, you ought to behave among them in such a way as not even to direct your thoughts to them, but must instead entirely ignore them, seeking to present your soul pure and intact to God, without being disturbed by thoughts of any sort."

We must be nourished entirely by all that is positive and pleasing to God. If we keep far from sin, we will eliminate the demonic presence and will no longer be afraid of the devil. The Bible for its part never tells us to fear the devil. Jesus was not afraid of the devil and did not teach His followers to fear him, even when one comes face-to-face with him. He casts out demons and teaches his own to do the same. But Jesus, as throughout the Bible, invites us to fear the works of Satan, the world, sin, and temptations. In the First Letter of St. Peter, chapter five, the apostle asks us to "Cast all your anxieties on him, for he cares about you. Be sober, be watchful. Your adversary the devil prowls around like a roaring lion, seeking someone to devour. Resist him, firm in your faith, knowing that the same experience of suffering is required of your brotherhood throughout the world. And after you have suffered a little while, the God of all grace, who has called you to his eternal glory in Christ, will himself restore, establish, and strengthen you." St. Paul echoes this in chapter six in the Letter to the Ephesians, reminding the faithful to "Be strong in the Lord and in the strength of his might. Put on the whole armor of God, that you may be able to stand against the wiles of the devil."

On one side, the devil seeks to devour us, while on the other God takes care of us, and through Christ has already prepared a place for us in eternal glory. *We have only to choose between sin or the grace to resist temptation. We must feel secure in God's aid, in the protection of Mary and our guardian angel. It is a sin to allow ourselves to be overtaken by desperation, the fruit of the temptation that would have us believe that evil is the true protagonist of history. We know that Jesus is the true protagonist of history. To choose Him distances evil from history, beginning with our own history.*

A concept which was quite clear to the prophets: "Do not fear, O Zion; let not your hands grow weak. The LORD your God is in your midst, a warrior who gives victory; he will rejoice over you with gladness, he will renew you in his love, he will exult over you with loud singing" (Zeph. 3:16–17). "In the end, my immaculate heart will triumph" was Our Lady's promise at the end of the prophecy of Fátima. For this reason and without mincing his words, St. Paul speaks of the joy, celebration, and peace that must characterize the Christian, in his Letter to the Philippians (4:4–7): "Rejoice in the Lord always; again I will say, Rejoice. Let all men know your forbearance. The Lord is at hand. Have no anxiety about anything, but in everything by prayer and supplication with thanksgiving let your requests be made known to God. And the peace of God, which passes all understanding, will keep your hearts and your minds in Christ Jesus."

Good will triumph. And if one wants to have an idea, however partial, of the omnipotence and grandeur of God, do like St. Bakhita and think of the starry sky. This image allows us to approach another fundamental concept already expressed by St. Paul: all the stars shine, but not with the same intensity. Both in Hell and in Heaven, we will not all be equal. In this sense, the vision provided in the Divine Comedy *is very realistic and the book of Revelation leads us to the same understanding in its description of the multitude of holy souls. All of us will be happy to share intimacy with God in Paradise, but not in the same way. "In His will is our peace," says Pia dei Tolomei to Dante, but the uniqueness of the human person remains. No one is the same as another, in earthly life as in eternal life. All of us, however, can contribute, each with our own strengths, whether great or small; we must simply use them. And as we read in the conclusion to chapter eleven of Matthew, we must never fear that we will not be able. Jesus goes out of his way to comfort those who cannot, those who are already crushed by heavy loads: "Come to me, all who labor and are heavy laden, and I will give you rest. Take my yoke upon you, and learn from me; for I am gentle and lowly in heart, and you will find rest for your souls. For my yoke is easy, and my burden is light."*

And so, if the Kingdom of God is not of this world, this does not mean that it cannot already be found within us and that we cannot make it a lived reality for those around us. Jesus Himself makes this explicit in His conduct. He is very attentive to the things of this world: He heals the sick and cultivates friendships. When He is tired and under duress, He goes to visit Lazarus and his sisters. Entering their house, He gladly stays to eat with them. He works for His living. He is very attentive to the needs of those near to Him and of those He meets along His way. As He tells in the parable of the Good Shepherd, He is ready to do anything in order to save the lost sheep. So too is He ready to celebrate when one who is lost returns home. Because "there will be more joy in heaven over one sinner who repents than over ninety-nine righteous persons who need no repentance" (Luke 15:7).

Everything is seen and lived in function of eternal life. The parable of the young rich man helps us to comprehend that life is a sort of itinerary divided into two parts, in which the first part, on earth, has the purpose of making us earn paradise in the second part. And Jesus is demanding and explicit in indicating the right path, as in Mark 8:34–36: "If any man would come after me, let him deny himself and take up his cross and follow me. For whoever would save his life will lose it; and whoever loses his life for my sake and the gospel's will save it. For what does it profit a man to gain the whole world and forfeit his life?" After His encounter with the young rich man, in the tenth chapter of Mark, Jesus announces a recompense for those who have left everything to follow Him. This does not mean that the Lord is contrary to terrestrial goods, but that He is against every form of human attachment to them. Which is the very essence of temptation and sin.

To resist we must be severe with ourselves, because as St. Catherine of Siena admonished, "our enemies never sleep, but are always on the watch to persecute us." For this reason, she invited the faithful to surrender self-love and "servile fears" with regard to earthly desires, "with a determined will, with patience, and with firm perseverance," to be able to be "manly knights capable of fighting against our enemies for love of Christ Crucified." Otherwise, "we will be so timid that even our shadow would frighten us."

Christianity lived in a manly and vigorous way allows us to close the doors to the devil. In his encyclical *Exuente iam anno*, Leo XIII wrote, "The whole essence of a Christian life is to reject the corruption of the world and to oppose constantly any indulgence in it." The world, as St. Augustine says, "besieges us" and exploits our weaknesses, and even our legitimate "fear of suffering." For this reason, Jesus invites us to be pure as doves, but also clever as snakes. Prudence and candor, interior strength and prayer, finding insight in the earthly experience of those who, like St. Augustine, do not disdain to ask, "Lord, help me in my struggle, help me to triumph over the snares of evil, substitute my weakness and, in the end, crown my fight with Your own victory."

Open Doors to the Devil

THE SLOW DEGRADATION OF the family is emblematic of the devil's action in society. The very fact that a well-formed family was the setting in which Jesus chose to be born and to grow makes it a privileged target. The family is under attack. Cultural changes, laws, work, the use of free time, mass media, all work against this fundamental and irreplaceable nucleus for the growth of new generations. These are all doors that are left open to the devil who, once he enters, even if we are not aware of it, erodes it from within, consumes, divides, destroys.

A fundamental case is the sudden evolution of female behaviors, generated not only by ideological motivations but also by contingent factors. Today, unfortunately, one wage-earner does not suffice for many families. How can one maintain a family with children when making less than a thousand euros per month? Women are now forced to enter the workforce to make ends meet, even those who would rather not. Even before, it was common for women to work. Agrarian society facilitated this, despite the many difficulties of running a family, envisioning for women forms of work together with their husbands and children. Even Our Lady had calloused hands, but she was able to still be a mother. She was certainly not the lovely lady we find on our prayer cards and statues. In today's reality, instead, it is difficult for women to work the entire day and then be fully a mom. Doing this requires enormous effort, total dedication, and much renunciation, with full collaboration between husband and wife. This is increasingly difficult to find among younger couples, because society itself urges them to live superficial relationships and to see sacrifice as useless. How many fathers have completely lost the pedagogical and educational sense of their paternity?

The dissolution of the family is often a result of this. Children are left alone. They do everything possible to acquire a convenient autonomy as early as possible. They sit alone in front of the TV or on the computer, and cultivate friendships beyond the interest of their parents, who have given up teaching and, no longer enforcing the rules with severity and firmness, have lost all authority. Naturally, it is impossible to return to the family model I knew as a child. Even then, there were adulterations and, in any case, too many things have changed. Considering only the evolution of the means of communication, we see everywhere how it has revolutionized our lifestyles. We do well to remember that in most families back then, the mothers were the cornerstone, the architects of their children's education. In families with many children, this type of education was even more effective because a child can easily hide what they do from their parents, but not so easily from their siblings. Women's emancipation was understood as conforming their behavior to male behavior. The result is that if before it was usually the husband who had erroneous attitudes toward education, now it is both man and woman. Instead of improving, we have gone backward.

If the women's liberation movement had exerted the same energy not to make women resemble men but to bring men to a fuller awareness of their family duties, to rediscover their life motivation within the family and in a peer relationship with women, the present situation of families would be quite different, and certainly women would have made gains in terms of authority and their role in society.

Here too, as always, we must consider the power of temptation that makes the easiest path seem the right one. And there are many stories about diabolical influence in the family setting, which help us to understand the provenance of this tension toward dissolution and the superficiality with which the new concept of the enlarged family is being disseminated, a model without respect for children, without any attention to their educational needs and to their affective needs, generating confusion in their heads and in their hearts, which often leads them into the offices of psychologists and psychiatrists, who are too often sentimentally ill-equipped and spiritually arid, and thus incapable of comprehending the extent and the nature of the problem.

How many families do we know that are irreparably destroyed by the capriciousness of temptations? But we have also heard of families undergoing harsh trials that nevertheless stay afloat in some way. Approaching these issues from the viewpoint of diabolical influences, it would seem that many ambivalent situations acquire obvious significance. *I am following a family that has been crushed by a woman connected to Satan, to whom the devil grants everything she asks. The husband of the couple in question receives messages, visits, and continual telephone calls from the woman and has fallen for her, despite the fact that he has often told her he wants to end the relationship. He continues to have strong feelings for his wife and children. He gladly came with his wife to see me. His is not a case of possession but of malign influence that keeps him enslaved. All the signs are there, including his loss of faith, which before held an important place in his life. At one point, he completely ended his relationship with God. Through the exorcisms, he is gradually rediscovering it. But the woman has not stopped tormenting him and he has not been able to be fully liberated. We began a difficult path of prayer with the wife. She understands him, has forgiven him, and both want to start over, fighting together against the stubbornness of the one who seeks to divide them.*

This is a family like many others, in which the devil has entered to destroy it through the fault of one of its components. If that husband had not conceded space to that temptation, the devil could not have done a thing. It is important always to be aware of the fact that the devil insinuates himself into the cracks, and to keep homes standing we must continually entrust them to God. If we forget God, we are immediately ready to justify every type of weakness and error.

If we forget God, we are very quick to place ourselves in the center of the universe. "No longer God, but me, me, me," as one of the visionaries of Medjugorje, Marja, pointed out in a television interview. And in these cases, it is almost always the family that pays the price. This is what happened to a couple that told their story on television in an interesting and unique documentary on love in Italy directed by Luigi Comencini in 1978. Both husband and wife spoke in front of the cameras of the Italian State Television Company (RAI), two simple people in their thirties.

The whole problem, she said, "began with my mother-in-law. When we got married, she went mad with jealousy. She didn't want her son to come live with me. I remember her yelling, 'He's mine, he's mine! He's flesh of my flesh. I gave birth to him!' After some time, I started having health problems that only grew worse, and I felt I no longer loved my husband. Someone who knew about our story recommended I go to an exorcist."

The husband then added, "The exorcisms gave her some peace but only for a day or two. Then it all began again. A group of charismatics then offered to come and pray in our home."

The woman said, "They began praying and the demon inside me shouted, 'I don't want to leave! I don't want to leave!' One day, after a terrible scream, I felt better. From that moment, my failing relationship with my husband began to improve. I once again felt all the love I had for him."

Good Can Come of Evil

Domenico ran on the sidewalk along the seashore. He was almost out of breath. From the station, the train had already given the signal for departure. It was the commuter train, the only one that morning for the main city. During the postwar emergency, his family had faced serious economic hardship. They were waiting for him to start a new job in the city. He could not miss this opportunity. The pay was not the best, but it was stable employment. They had even promised him an advance on the first month's wages. For his mother, debilitated by depravations, and for his two younger brothers, it would be a return to a dignified life. Domenico was running late, or maybe the train was ahead of schedule. His mother had caused him to lose precious time sewing his frayed shirt collar. As soon as she had finished, he took off running. He took from the coat rack the only men's jacket in the house, which had been his father's, and ran off.

From the station he could see the train puffing out smoke from the boiler as it departed. Though aware he had missed the train he kept running. His mother had assured him of her prayers that all would turn out well. And when that saintly woman promised prayers, things always turned out for the best. He reached the ramp leading up to the platform when the train was already moving. At the top of those twenty meters, he could see the last car disappearing into the tunnel. He was sweating, tired, and overcome by a veil of desperation that clouded his eyes. He had missed the train, lost a job, and lost the daily bread for his brothers.

He stopped a moment at the top of the ramp instead of returning back down it and chose to take the longer route home. When he passed by the station director's booth, his mother came to mind, doubtless with her rosary in hand, before the image of Our Lady, hanging above the kitchen table. Domenico was thinking of those useless prayers when he heard someone calling from behind him. It was the old parish priest. He too had climbed the ramp to the platform. He was to take the train that would depart in the opposite direction in a few minutes. Seeing the boy's face wet with tears, he approached to ask the reason for his sadness. Domenico had always been a boy of few words, but the few words were enough: "I found a job, but I missed the train."

The priest knew the family situation, similar to many families in the town at any rate. He approached to console him. With his arm around his shoulders, he walked some paces to the stairs that returned to the street, and before leaving him to cross the tracks and await his train, said to him: "Don't worry. Your mother is always there praying. She knows with certainty: good can come from evil."

Domenico descended the stairs. He stopped at the fourth or fifth stair. The thought of his mother praying filled him with anguish, and from the priest's words he could find no hope. When he returned home, however, he was like an overflowing river. His mother, seated at the table under the image of Our Lady, had reached her fourth rosary. She thought he was in the city at his job interview and was stunned to see him home so soon. As he told his story of missing the train he was strangely overcome by uncontainable joy.

"Fr. Giacomo told me that good can come of evil."

His mother raised her eyes to Our Lady. Her son, as well as her husband, had never had any predilection for things of the Church. The fact that he came home quoting this phrase from the priest with so much enthusiasm seemed to her to be a grace. Instead of a job, Our Lady had helped him discover the faith. The boy insisted: "It was as if Fr. Giacomo had seen things before they happened. I descended the stairs from the station and turning the corner I ran into Maria. For months I had been trying to speak with her but couldn't find the courage. We talked from the station all the way home. About everything, Mama. We talked about everything. And it seemed like it wasn't even the first time, and that we had already discussed some things. When we parted, we still had a thousand things to tell each other."

The two of them eventually got married, had children, and made a little fortune in a big city. Their simple story was told by Domenico at the celebration of their fiftieth wedding anniversary in his spontaneous way of expressing himself, and with the many words that he did not have but which he had discovered in his long life with Maria. Recalling Fr. Giacomo's words and the fact that his mother "surely knew," he glanced at their many grandchildren and friends united for the party, and could not withhold his tears.

"Before my eyes," he said as he squeezed the hand of his wife resting on the table, "is yet another of the many confirmations that good can come from evil."

This true story tells us that God's grace can enlighten any situation, even the darkest and saddest. *We must desire it with all our strength, ask for it through prayer. Only in this way can one experience being reborn to new life through the strong desire to fight evil with good and with forgiveness. I once had contact with families that were hard pressed by evil, but by pursuing the good with firm dedication, have become the fulcrum of a moral and spiritual renewal among their friends and even throughout entire communities.*

For many years, Fr. Candido was exorcising a young woman without apparent benefit. When he died, I continued exorcising her every week. At the time, I was still not well-known and could reserve Tuesday morning for this particularly serious case. I often went to her home in a town outside of Rome on the via Cassia.

One day, going there by car, I was particularly demoralized. I spoke with Rosa, the woman who always accompanied me, of the difficult situation we were going to confront and of the fact that despite the consistent number of exorcisms, we still were not able to resolve it. She had had, it is true, some small benefit. Every time she was exorcised she felt better. But after several days, she would suffer a worsening, a sort of recharge of the demonic. She suffered terrible headaches that made it impossible for her to do anything. I must confess that these thoughts caused me to go there that day with less motivation than usual. Naturally we did not say this to her. After the exorcism, of her own initiative, she began telling us: "Fr. Amorth, you surely do not know that no one has ever gone to church in my family. Ever since I have had this problem, though, I have been inviting them to the prayer seeking God's help and the intercession of Our Lady, and now my brothers and their families have been attending church regularly, going to Mass, and praying together as husband and wife."

These words led me to consider the case in a new light. I realized that in all those years the union between her and her husband had gone to ruin. But now it seemed stronger than ever. My heart opened. I thought how at times it seems the exorcisms fail to obtain any results and then you find out that the collateral graces are much more important than the liberation of that person from the devil. We just need the humility to understand this.

Fifteen years have passed since I assisted her. She continues to go to an exorcist friend. He too is a disciple of Fr. Candido. The improvement continues, but she always needs to be helped through exorcisms and the prayer of all her friends and acquaintances, which has become increasingly assiduous. The truth is that quite often the Lord can make use of an illness or even a case of possession to grant enormous graces, which can have value for eternity and therefore a much greater value than a healing or liberation. In Lourdes, I met people who thanked God for their uncurable diseases. They made of them an instrument to implore the conversion of sinners. We seek miracles of healing. We go to Lourdes with them, because we are so tied to earthly things that we can touch, hear, and see. We cannot detach ourselves from them. At times the Lord wants to be with us in our weakness and give us the grace we are asking. Many other times, however, he considers other graces, spiritual and not material ones, to be better for us.

I'll never forget the case of an exorcist that involved an entire parish. It concerned a girl who had been cursed. She too suffered terrible headaches and stomachaches that prevented her from doing any activity. It was a sort of total disability. We began with the exorcisms. Her relatives asked the parish priest to pray. He got a parish group involved, asking for their prayers at Sunday Mass, and gradually, the entire parish felt called to pray for her. They did novenas, Rosaries, communal prayers, and were able to obtain her liberation after a few years. And when a liberation comes about in such short time, I jump for joy, even at my venerable age.

In Wonderland

Who made man? If we remove our origin in God we can no longer comprehend anything. It is essential to recognize God as the foundation of all things, of all thoughts, of all actions. If God is removed, man is factually destroyed, he remains a degenerate, subject to his whims and to ethical relativism.

This is the fundamental problem: to place or not to place God above all things. To consider oneself or not to consider oneself in all matters dependent on the grace of God. *The story of the "Distracted Frog" sheds light on this. Written by the Danish author Johannes Joergensen, it is a parable for children that teaches them the roots of evil and its consequences.*

"It was a beautiful September morning. All the meadows sparkled with the dew and the Mary's yarn, bright as if it were silk, fluctuating in the breeze. It came from far away and travelled far away. One of those threads landed in a treetop and the pilot, a little black and yellow spider, left its weightless ship and alighted on the resistant ground of a leaf. But he was content with that place. He then went to a large, thorny hedge, where there were branches and sprouts in abundance to weave his thread upon. And the spider immediately got to work, using the long thread on which he had descended to hold the highest point of his web.

"It became a large, beautiful web. It had something particular about it: one could say it was spun into thin air without being able to see what held the upper edge of it. One needs good eyes to see the thread of a spider's web.

"Days came and days went. The flies began to be scarce and the spider was forced to enlarge his web. The thread spanned high and wide and the thin web soon covered the entire hedge. The shiny dewdrops of the humid October mornings hanging from it made it look like a tulle embroidered with pearls. The spider was proud of her work. She was no longer that poor little spider that swung in the air attached by a thread, without a penny in her pocket, so to speak, and without any other worldly goods than the glands than spun her filaments. Now she was a heavy and important spider, well-provisioned and possessing the biggest web in the hedge.

"One morning she awoke in a terribly strange mood. There had been a frost that night and there was not the least ray of sunlight to gladden the earth, not even the smallest fly buzzing in the air. The spider was left hungry and unemployed the whole autumn day. Bored, she made the rounds on her web to see if it needed repairs by chance. She pulled at every thread, attentive that each one was nice and tight. But although she found it all in order, she was still in a terrible mood. In the end, she noticed at the far edge of her web, a thread that seemed completely new.

"All the other threads went this way and that, and the spider knew every branch to which they were attached. That inexplicable thread went nowhere and so she concluded it went straight into the air. The spider rose on her hind legs and looked upward with all of her eyes, but could not understand where it ended up. The more she looked in vain, the more she grew angry.

"She had forgotten that one calm September day, she had descended on that very thread. Nor could she recall how very useful that thread had been in helping her spin and enlarge her web. She simply thought it was a stupid, good-for-nothing thread that was not attached to anything but went right out into a void. She decided to cut it with one swift blow of her teeth. At that moment, the entire web gave out. The entire web, so artistically created, collapsed. When the spider came to her senses, she found herself on the leaves of the thorny hedge, wrapped in the ruins of her web

that had become a little wet rag. One little instant was all it took to destroy her magnificent home, simply because she did not understand the utility of the 'thread from above.'"

Man is the cause of his own evil. The diabolical intervention is perceptible in that state of distress that pervades the spider at the height of her success. One of the absolute masterpieces of world literature comes to mind when thinking of fables and fairy tales: *Pinocchio* by Collodi. The entire human predicament is encapsulated in that very simple tale which has many times been the subject of theological readings. Consider Geppetto as God the Creator, or Mangiafuoco as Satan, or the Fairy with Turquoise Hair as the Virgin Mary, and so forth. Pinocchio is obviously a man like the rest of us. He is not wicked, but he is surrounded by evil, corrupted by bad company, deceived by the colorful ornaments of temptations. And it is easy to think of toyland as the real deception of our time, if we consider the many analogous settings in literature: there is, for example, the land of Bengodi that deceives the ingenuous in Boccaccio's *Decameron*; or Sugarcandy Mountain, which fools the entire population in Orwell's *Animal Farm*. These are places where one goes with the mirage of all-inclusive entertainment. *Far from God and from the teachings of the one who loves us, one is alienated by the absolute lack of moral reference points and ends up losing one's humanity, risking one's hide like Pinocchio, a modern-day Jonah, in the belly of the whale, and with it risking one's soul. At that point, only recourse to the merciful help of Mary can raise us toward the fullness of our being as creatures — in other words, in God's image and likeness.*

God is the beginning. When we remove the beginning, the end no longer makes sense, and everything collapses. Without Him, the only existence possible is one of desperation or that of the homo hominis lupus. *This is true also of all the great accomplishments of humanity. Remove*

God and they count for nothing. Think of the three principals of the French Revolution: liberty, equality, and fraternity. All three are fundamentally Christian, based on divine teaching. Once God was removed, they produced mounds of corpses. Analogously, when He who animates Christian principles is removed, everything is removed. What remains are simple anthropological and humanitarian foundations that can only produce injustice and ruin.

A Life of Death

The observation that emerges from this analysis is that we need God more than anything else. Ours is an extreme need for God. The individual needs God, the family needs God, society needs God. In his very modern reading of current society, Pius XII sustained that "the greatest sin of our age is that man has lost his sense of sin." Putting aside God, one becomes insensible to sin and the boundaries between good and evil, between right and wrong, even between human and inhuman become increasingly evanescent.

A recent advertising campaign against the nasty habit of abandoning pets is in some ways emblematic. In the images and expressions used, man's actions were compared to those of animals, saying that men behave like beasts and that animals are better than men, as many animal-rights activists affirm. The problem lies in the fact that society proclaims its indignation over the abandonment of a dog, but creates everyday thousands and millions of events that have as their direct consequences the destruction of nature. And it is the same society that does not grow indignant, but rather finds it politically correct, to justify the suppression of a human being through euthanasia. One might ask why the same commitment to fight and to spend money on advertising against the abandonment of pets is not spent to counter the plague of the abandonment of the elderly. Dogs end up in kennels, the elderly in retirement homes, and at times, there is little difference. And yet, there is always a popular personality who will defend the cause of animals.

The aim is noble, indeed it is even Christian, but there is no less nobility in publicly defending abandoned persons.

It is a shoddy formation that guides the actions of most of the media. *These are the paradoxes to which the deliberate rejection of every spiritual reference point leads. And not even the common distinction between good guys and bad guys is acceptable. What really makes the difference is if and where we place God in our lives. Consider the terrible suppression of children in their mothers' wombs. Abortions registered around the world are calculated at about thirty-two million per year. This is an astonishing number. It is a form of mass self-annihilation that society has easily learned to justify, inserting it into the category of the politically correct. Consider the "morning-after pill," the pill that provokes a supposed chemical abortion, RU-486. The defense of it, on the grounds that fetuses do not feel pain, leaves unaltered the substance of the matter: they are human beings with souls created in the image and likeness of God from the moment of their conception. "The Angel of the Lord announced unto Mary and she conceived by the power of the Holy Spirit. . . . And the Word became flesh and dwelt among us. And when Elizabeth heard the greeting of Mary, the babe leaped in her womb; and Elizabeth was filled with the Holy Spirit and she exclaimed with a loud cry, 'Blessed are you among women, and blessed is the fruit of your womb! And why is this granted to me, that the mother of my Lord should come to me?'" (Luke 1:41–43). Suppressing a fetus is suppressing a human being.*

God is the God of life. Satan, rejecting God, is for death. And wherever death is, his action is present. "Sin is crouching at the door; its desire is for you, but you must master it" (Gen. 4:7). Death came into the world through the work of the devil, who convinced man to betray God's plan like he did. A concept that is at the heart of Christian teaching and cannot be forgotten: "If you eat of this you shall die." Christ came to vanquish death. We are the image and likeness of God in the totality of our soul and body.

Christ's first victory was His victory over death. His second victory was over the dissolution of the body. His third victory was to open the gates of Paradise, which had been closed and guarded by angels after the expulsion from the Garden of Eden. Christ rose from the dead, descended to the underworld, and gives us back our hope of Heaven and entrusts the keys to Peter: the angels are no longer the guardians, but a man who is at the gates to welcome us. A sign of immense availability, a road paved for salvation. Logically, the devil will do all he can to prohibit his imminent defeat.

God created us for eternal life; the devil brought death; Christ triumphed over death. If we remove God from our lives the fate that awaits us is the devil, perdition, Hell — in other words, the definitive separation from God and therefore death. If we welcome God in our lives, as Mary did in her womb, our destiny is in the eternity of joy. As Origen explained, "Life is a battle in which the soldiers of Satan battle with the soldiers of God." Sooner or later, he added, "a man endowed with reason" must choose which side he is on. Many centuries later, a former soldier named Ignatius of Loyola made famous in his *Spiritual Exercises* the same concept, indicating for each of us the necessity of choosing to rally behind one of the two flags.

In reality, however, it seems that man is constantly searching for an escape from death. There are two epitaphs in the beautiful American collection of poems, the *Spoon River Anthology,* that perfectly represent the human desire for subjugation and death, even if at different levels of perversity. On the tombstone of John M. Church, one reads:

> I was attorney for the "Q"
> And the Indemnity Company which insured
> The owners of the mine.
> I pulled the wires with judge and jury,
> And the upper courts, to beat the claims
> Of the crippled, the widow and orphan,

And made a fortune thereat.
The bar association sang my praises
In a high-flown resolution.
And the floral tributes were many—
But the rats devoured my heart
And a snake made a nest in my skull.

An unbridled, useless race for power and money. So too did the diabolical perversity of the deceased Robert Davidson turn out to be fruitless, by his own admission:

I grew spiritually fat living off the souls of men.
If I saw a soul that was strong
I wounded its pride and devoured its strength.
The shelters of friendship knew my cunning,
For where I could steal a friend I did so.
And wherever I could enlarge my power
By undermining ambition, I did so,
Thus to make smooth my own.
And to triumph over other souls,
Just to assert and prove my superior strength,
Was with me a delight,
The keen exhilaration of soul gymnastics.
Devouring souls, I should have lived forever.
But their undigested remains bred in me a deadly nephritis.

History is full of the deadly effects of the devil's work. When excesses of perfidy and malice are reached that cannot be humanly explained through the normal logic of sentiments, it means that an extra-human force has pulled them to excesses. The Holocaust, Stalin's purges, the slave trade, mothers who kill their children, a father who exterminates his family and then kills himself. There are also many episodes that date far back, before Christianity, that cannot be explained without considering the influence of a "perverted and perverting" being, as Paul VI called him, that has enabled those things to happen.

Consider the slave trade. One of the darkest pages of human history, in which even many of the most important people were embroiled in various time periods. The African peoples were divided up like Christ's tunic among the great Western nations, the Arab world, and the Turks. And not only in Africa: many Asian peoples were also subject to deportation into slavery.

The role of a great saint of our times such as Giuseppina Bakhita is quite interesting in this regard. *I had the good fortune of meeting her when I was a child because she came to my school to tell her story. My memory of her is indelible ever since that day.* An African from the Sudan, she was kidnapped when only a few years old by Arab traffickers, who sold her to a Turkish general. That began for her a life of abuse and violence, until an Italian diplomat in the Sudan decided to redeem her and bring her to Italy, entrusting her as a nanny to a friend in Veneto. There, Bakhita met Christ, manifested her firm desire to follow Him, and became a Canosian Sister. Through her life of sanctity, she transformed the hatred and violence she suffered into an inexhaustible wellspring of love. She forgave everything, including her kidnappers and those who barbarously abused her: she wanted to embrace them and thank them, because without them she would never have come to know Jesus Christ.

Thanks to this disposition for Jesus, an insignificant African slave, a humble nun without any education became an endless source of love for millions of people who throughout the world have entrusted themselves to her intercession, without racial, cultural, or even religious distinction. The Sudanese sister is perhaps the only example of a saint capable of being a bridge with the Islamic world, as well as between the West and sub-Saharan Africa. To her, hatred and subjugation are defeated by love, death by the joy of living. Inspired by God, as she herself always insisted, she journeyed since her infancy along the only road that exists for defeating Satan and all evil that assails us during our earthly sojourn. It is the miracle we encountered in the story of Domenico: through trust in the Lord, evil is transformed into good.

He Who Desires Death

One day, St. Francis left his cell at La Verna wanting to pray in solitude. He chose a stone on the rocky crag "overlooking a cliff from an enormous height," as we read in *The Considerations on the Stigmata*. It was "a horrible and frightening precipice. The devil came immediately with a great storm and crash, in terrible form, striking him to cast him down. St. Francis could flee nowhere but could not bear the horrible sight of the devil, and thus turned to the rock with his hands and with his face and with all his body, pleading to God, and groping with his hands for anything to cling to. But as pleased God, who never tempts His servants more than they can bear, immediately the rock he was grasping opened according to the form of his body and in such a way as if he had placed hands and face in melted wax, that this rock took the form of his face and hands and, aided by God, survived the onslaught of the devil."

Men of God have many experiences of death provoked by the devil. Some of them were harshly tried even with temptations to commit suicide. The story of the Servant of God Fr. Semeria comes to mind, when he was a military chaplain at the front in the First World War. After the first months of fighting, exhausted by blood and human ferocity, and persecuted by members of the hierarchy, he collapsed physically and psychologically under the weight of a feeling of uselessness and a sense of guilt for his previous patriotic and interventionist opinions. This is similar to what many Italian priests of that period went through, among whom was Fr. Primo Mazzolari.

Devastated by depression, Semeria was aided by friends and taken to Switzerland for cures. There he suffered a true Gethsemane: the horror for blood spilt, the weight of his guilt, his faith that vacillated. But at the same time he found the strength to continue. For fear he might take his life, his standard-issue gun was taken from him. He recalled how he suffered on several occasions the temptation to commit suicide, and how he wandered entire nights on train tracks waiting to be run over by a train. Then, slowly, with the help of friends and through prayer, divine grace began to illumine once more the lamp of faith in him. The man who came out of this crisis was a new man, totally dedicated to God and to the needs of his neighbor, who then set off on the path of the Cross and of sanctity.

The devil is the one who desires death, who has constructed for himself and for his friends a kingdom of death. Not by accident do satanic cults practice human sacrifice to celebrate Satan, to verify the union with him of his adepts. Just like the Black Masses celebrated on the body of a sexually humiliated woman, the affront to life and to its conception is obvious. The devil pursues his objective of death with the aim of eternal damnation. Death is understood as the destruction of life.

The great works of the devil are wars. The devil foments wars, just as he foments the culture of death that leads to abortion, euthanasia, and the contraceptive culture that produces a growing number of couples who deliberately choose not to have children. Then there are killers who choose to kill as a profession, terrorists, and kamikaze who use death as an instrument in a religious, ideological, or political war.

The destruction of the World Trade Center in New York — here, Fr. Amorth did not hide a grimace of horror — *must be interpreted as a great work of the devil. For him, it was a sort of show of power. Not because he gains power by doing harm, but because evil and death are expressions of his opposition to God. Death is the realization of his personality as a denier of life, of his hatred for all that is love and for all God's creatures. His is a hatred of God to the point of self-hatred.*

A terrible trait that is found in all those who follow him: A will to destruction that is constantly carried out in daily life, in the effort to destroy families, civil society, and nations. *How many people, how many communities of believers are constantly threatened by genocide, how many are forced to flee from their lands!* The massacres in Rwanda come to mind, as well as those in Sudan, the repression in Tibet and in the former Soviet Union, the repeated attacks on the Kurds, the persecution and killing of Christians in Africa and Asia. If one looks back through the years and centuries, the list would be interminable. *Where there is killing and bloodshed there is always the work of the devil. Wars have always been caused and inspired by the devil. It is so true that even curses are almost always marked by this tenacious quest for death.*

A doctor came to me one day. He raised the hem of his pants to show me his legs. They were marked by scars from numerous surgeries. Then he began to tell his story. His father was from Calabria and had decided to study law, although his mother had insisted he become a priest. He did not feel called to the priesthood, but not able to convince her that his path was a different one, he was forced to leave Calabria. He got married and became an important lawyer. He had children, but continued to suffer contention with his mother and the bitterness she harbored toward him. Despite this, his life continued to move forward in the best of ways. One day a picture was taken of their youngest son, who would later become a doctor. It was a very sweet image in which the eight-year-old child was shown wearing shorts, according to the fashion of that time. The lawyer thought the tenderness of that image might have a positive effect on the feelings of his mother. He decided to send this picture of a grandson to his grandmother.

What happened next was devastating. In a letter, the mother responded to this tender attempt at reconciliation with two sentences of absolute malice: "May this boy's legs be forever tormented with sickness. If you return to Calabria you will die in the bed you were born in."

The child grew and began to have pain in his legs that grew worse over the years. Surgical interventions were sought. The lawyer, suffering for the curse inflicted by his mother, sought the help of exorcists. In the meantime, the lawyer's mother died. Remembering her curse, he decided not to attend the funeral. After a few years, a close friend from his childhood also died. At that point, the lawyer, who had never returned home, decided it was right to go, pressured by his friend's wife. Of course, he had no intention of setting foot in his parents' house. He went by train. The moment he arrived he fell gravely ill and did not regain consciousness. His friends, who knew nothing about this story, assisted him and naturally took him to his father's house. That night he died, in the very bed in which he was born.

An incredible story that confirms some of the fundamental aspects concerning curses, which we have dealt with already. *Quite often, the malevolent effect continues even after the death of the one who made the curse. At times, curses are so strong that exorcisms have no decisive effect on them. This illustrates the fundamental truth that the devil is always the one who seeks death: the death of soul or body, if not both.*

Far from God, the Good Is a Deception

From the very beginning, the Bible presents the devil as the one who opposes God and as the tempter of man, always seeking to make him fall. In the Gospel, we see Jesus, who casts out demons in cases of possession. At various points in Scripture, other diabolical evils are mentioned as well, manifested with negative influence in the work and life of men. This principle was emphasized also at the Second Vatican Council, in *Gaudium et Spes*: "For a monumental struggle against the powers of darkness pervades the whole history of man. The battle was joined from the very origins of the world and will continue until the last day, as the Lord has attested."

Through sin, the devil seeks to distance man from God and lead him to Hell. He knows our weak points to perfection. Every man, furthermore, is born with Original Sin. We are already persons wounded by sin. We carry it within us, as if it were written into our genes. We have natural tendencies that are negative, which do not emerge directly from the devil but are an intrinsic part of our nature. Such tendencies must be held in check if we want to live in and build stable relations with others. The devil exploits these tendencies. He constantly invites us to unleash them, making us believe that only in this way can we reach our full realization and freedom.

This action is made obvious in society, in the way in which it is organized and has evolved culturally. There has been a progressive assertion of psychological, psychoanalytical, and philosophical theories stating that a person who wants to be truly himself and affirm his own personality must free his impulses, not control them or "repress" them, as one prefers to say now with this intentionally negative term. Self-control is acceptable only in what is considered politically incorrect, which is a limit that is constantly moved forward as society gradually grows habituated to the latest moral conquests of modernity. Therefore, a green light to all that pertains to sexual behavior, contraception, the purely egoistical affirmation of one's self, to pleasure and to unbridled hedonism, to climbing the career ladder at work or in politics, to consumerism, to the ruin of entire families by crazy purchases and running up debt only for the mirage of living beyond one's means.

We spoke about our weaknesses and the relative temptations. *The Sacred Scriptures are quite clear and we have seen this in numerous testimonies: we always have, in whatever circumstances, the instruments to overcome them. At the same time, it is clear that a person who renounces drawing near to God cannot resist, because he has no truly valid reason for doing so or (to be quite honest) it is not convenient for him. For this reason, the devil always seeks to distract us from God and from a life of prayer. For this reason, he seeks to put us in the company of people who will lead us far from God. At times he even makes use of the invitation to draw near to religious practices, for the sake of curiosity.*

We would need to dedicate an enormous amount of space for debating this specific topic with its many nuances, and the degrees of temptations connected to dabbling in other forms of religion and worship — in particular, the multitude of practices tied to Eastern philosophies, whose founding logic is so far from the truth we find in Jesus Christ, and all of which are bound up in theories of reincarnation.

In recent decades, the so-called New Age movement has widely disseminated these theories. *Consider reiki healing, which is based on the divinization of man, which coopts the forces of nature and uses them. The idea of chakras is likewise contrary to Christian Faith and even dangerous, because it opens to occult worlds where it is quite easy to encounter the evil one. I have always been very severe in my judgment on this point, because through chakra one can really open the gates to the abyss. Very rarely do those who subject themselves to these practices really know what they are doing. Those involved in reiki as well as those open to chakra invoke mysterious powers using formulas and words whose actual meanings remain hidden, often even to the teacher who pronounces them.*

Many throughout the years have attempted to drag Christ into these things, trying to separate practice from theory and the religious philosophies that inspire them. The risk is that the opposite occurs, however, as I have often had the chance to observe — much more so in periods when people are particularly disoriented in their ability to distinguish good from evil. In reality, every time there is a comingling, a mixing of Christianity with Eastern-styled beliefs, enormous harm ensues.

In these cases, the devil's work shows up clearly, his work in distancing us from Christ. This happens every time heresies arise in the Church. The initial idea seems good, innovating, but then it creates distance from communion, from the truth in Jesus Christ. *Perhaps because it is linked to a period in which I was a young man, but I always cite the example of the working-class priests. Their intention to live with factory workers and share their work in the factories to draw near to them and comprehend their real needs, though positive in some cases, often translated into the priest's distancing himself from ecclesial communion and in his drawing near to Marxism.*

We spoke of reincarnation. Eastern philosophies say that man, once he dies, reincarnates, lives a new life. He does not necessarily become another man, but he can become an animal, or even a plant, in a sort of repetition of a circular path of death and reincarnation that has as its final objective the annihilation of the self, of the person, in favor of a return into nothing, totally deprived of relations, a state called *nirvana*, which constitutes true liberation.

This is very far from the Christian conception of death and resurrection, where the person is not annihilated into nothing, but is fully realized in the One who is full realization Himself. If on one side liberation is the canceling of relationships and sentiments, on the other it is fulfilled in love, which by definition is relational. As Benedict XVI explained in a reflection found in the volume *Images of Hope*, "The Christian alternative to nirvana is the Trinity, that final unity in which the I and the thou are not diminished when they stand before one another, but compenetrate intimately in the Holy Spirit. . . . God did not create the person that it might be annihilated, but that it might open in all its height and all its extreme depth, there where the Holy Spirit embraces it and is the unity among diverse persons."

This path is one Jesus shows us on the Cross, because, as Benedict XVI explains in that volume, the Cross embraces the world and has its roots in the world. Above all, "from the cross the world draws its upward movement toward freedom and the breadth of God's promises. The cross brings about a new dynamic: the circle that spins in vain and eternally around the same point, the useless movement of the eternal return, is in this way broken. The cross that draws upward is the hook by which God lifts the entire world up to his height. Now the trajectory of history and human life is no longer circular but rises: it has received a destination and ascends with Christ into the hands of God."

This is what distinguishes Eastern philosophies from Christianity. And this cannot be considered a mere trifle. This difference contains the exclusive love of Christ for each human being, considered in his uniqueness and totality, because made in the image and likeness of God. In this difference we find the contrast between eternal life and eternal obliteration, between what unites and what separates, between the love of God and the deceit of the devil. One cannot in any way believe in reincarnation as a Christian. Precisely as concerns love, Christianity is the only religion that preaches charity, forgiveness, and mercy. There are those that preach peace, those that preach non-violence. But there is not one that proposes as its model forgiveness and mercy in the active sense of the term, as a concrete movement toward the other, of the I toward the thou.

This is the moral daily bread of the Christian. The movement of the I toward the thou is at the origin of the family, for example, and we Christians know that a family cannot continue to grow in love if forgiveness does not enter to heal disputes at their root. Without the daily exercise of forgiveness, without the reciprocal movement of the I toward the thou, couples fall apart, love becomes deception.

Abortion: The Devil's Triumph

One of Satan's triumphs was to bring it about that Catholic nations would accept laws permitting abortion. To make legal (almost praiseworthy in some cases, and not merely from medical necessity) the murder of the most defenseless of human beings: nothing could be more perverse. And to put their consciences in order, they even established the hour and the day before which that child is not a child but only a blob of cells. The person is reduced to butcher's meat like that which was burned in the gas ovens, like that of slaves exploited unto death for personal gain, or of the soldiers sent with absolute certainty to die in battle during the First World War. A work of leading consciences astray founded on deception which submits the life of a human being to the free choice of the woman; that subjugates the unobtainable life of a man, his right to have and construct a future to the power and the incontestable will of another man; that establishes that the life of a fetus is not true life until the ninetieth day of its existence , but only from the next day on. A deception as subtle as it is obvious and out in the open. Just think of the prologue of the law that affirms that life must be protected: "The state guarantees the right to conscientious and responsible procreation, it recognizes the social value of maternity and safeguards human life from its beginning."

It is the biggest crime of our society, due to the simple fact that it has been rendered legitimate. A clear contradiction if one considers the just motivations that urge us to implore an international moratorium on the death penalty. It is written that "If anyone slays Cain, vengeance shall be taken on him sevenfold" (Gen. 4:15), but before that it is written that no one should have killed Abel, the innocent one: "The voice of your brother's blood is crying to me from the ground" (Gen. 4:10). So many children are systematically and cynically killed. Scientific investigations have proven that those poor fetuses suffer, that they are conscious of death, they draw back, they contract, they seek to flee.

There is much to fear in the face of such a concentration of sins. The mercy of God is infinite, but when sins accumulate and concentrate ever more, consciences and entire societies harden, become proud and no longer recognize their errors.

As justification for this, they often cite the girl who is too young to become a mother in a society like ours, where at that age she should only be thinking of having fun and then, when it's okay, she gets married in her thirties. Besides the superficiality of the reasoning that often, though not explicitly, contrasts having fun with the life of a human being, I can say with absolute certainty in the light of my experience that abortion is a sin for which a woman is rarely able to forgive herself. I have always had great difficulty with the women who have repented after having killed the child in their womb. How can you restore what cannot be restored? We must start a journey with them. For the rest of their lives they must offer prayers of repentance, prayers for those who brought them to that decision, and do acts of charity in expiation. But many are not able to overcome the trauma. And the lack of forgiveness toward themselves is another sin that often leads to depression, if not to folly and even suicide.

I remember the last days of life of a woman obsessed by the continuous vision of the faces of thirteen children. She could not resist the thought of her thirteen abortions. And do not think this was an isolated case due to the repetition of this act. Naturally, the opposite occurs as well: after the second or the third abortion, killing can became habitual. More or less the same as happens with murderers. For years, I had to accompany spiritually with exorcisms a young married woman. She wanted children, but when she got pregnant she felt she was too young and still wanted to have fun. Her doctor convinced her to have an abortion. Just like the devil, the doctor managed to corrupt her conscience, convincing her of pre-packaged justifications and excuses for what she was about to do, telling herself that it was not yet a child, that she was certainly not the first woman to do this, that there would be no consequences for her, that she would not feel any pain and would not notice a thing. A devastating consultation.

Quite often it is family members, a boyfriend or husband, who convince the woman. The enormous weight of instigating homicide falls on the consciences of these people, and for the mother-to-be only desperation. To comprehend the suffering of these women it suffices to read some of the thousands of publications, great or small, that abound throughout the world, in which mothers who have had abortions tell of their experience and the difficulties they had, even for those with faith, to recover serenity, dignity, mental health, and the courage to ask for forgiveness and to forgive themselves, to look in the mirror, or to look their children in the face.

These words weighed like a millstone and continued to resound in the room as Fr. Gabriele stood up to go to the table where, with the usual modest disorder, various publications were to be found. He grabbed four or five booklets and offered them to me. They were stories of women who were willing to tell of their immense pain. "From Illusion to Truth," "I Was Dead Along with My Child," "I Found Forgiveness" were just some of the titles. I took them and leafed through them. From page 33 of a yellow book, I read aloud, "The doctor gave me the anesthetic. When I awoke, I was no longer the same person. They killed that child, and I died with her."

Legalized abortion is a true conquest of the devil. The morning-after pill is a terrible deception: it poisons and kills the child. The doctor, who by profession must heal, acts to kill, uses medicine to kill. They gave that pill the name "medicine," but medicines are for curing, not for killing. We stand before one of the many terrible cases in which they use a word, a strategy, a philosophical construct to justify or to facilitate murder or any other grave sin. In this setting, the indifference of people in the face of what is the worst and most atrocious plays a role.

But not only abortion. There is not only the indifference of those who instead of helping to save a life make themselves accomplices to killing it. There are killers who do not use guns, medicines, bombs, or knives. There are many ways to kill that often are not even considered as such. *One can kill a person even just psychologically. Examples of such cases are infinite. We can criticize a person in front of everyone and make them terribly uncomfortable and fill them with shame. Through the weapons of denigration, we can prevent a person from holding their head high, they can be killed emotionally and morally before their relatives, depriving them of their authority in the eyes of their children. Even worse results can be obtained through calumny and slander. And the* First Letter of St. John *is most severe on this matter: "He who hates his brother is a murderer."*

It is truly difficult to state that many of these cases are not downright homicides. There are men and women whose lives have been completely destroyed by physical and psychological violence. Often, and this is even worse, it provokes in them the temptation to commit suicide: to kill their bodily existence to escape those who are killing their soul. One homicide can cancel another homicide. And then there are so many people who choose to kill themselves slowly, in their spirit, suffocating all their emotions, their aspirations, and their impulses. A life without joy and without hope. It is the triumph of the devil, who is capable of hiding from man the mercy of God, His infinite goodness, His forgiveness, His desire to embrace anyone who might want His embrace, the joy experienced in trusting oneself to Providence.

At the root of it all is always the sin of pride, superbia, *both in the one who commits the evil and in the one who suffers it without seeing the way out. And then there are those to whom evil becomes a habit, those who do evil and would like to continue down that path, those who cannot get enough of it. There are hitmen, serial killers, and those who convince themselves that killing is right, that there are religious or moral motives that can justify the murderer. And the devil is always there inciting and convincing them that the evil action is not that serious, that there is no need to do good because there is always someone ready to hurt you, and so forth. If there are, however, glimmers of morality at the bottom of one's soul, teachings received as a child that still create resistance along the path of sin, it is enough to insinuate that those ideas have been overcome as completely useless bigotry, because real life is something else.*

This is the work of subversion and homogenization, which is above all the fruit of the environment in which one lives. A sick society generates sick children, sick institutions, bad teachers who are experts in the arts of spinning lies. *Corruption works in the depths. Consider the referendums in Italy on abortion and divorce. The beguiling and deceptive work of the devil acted upon many Catholics who voted based on reasoning that was structured more or less in this way: I would never accept to divorce my spouse and I would never have an abortion, but why should I prevent those from doing so who do not share my principles? Who am I to judge those living in terrible personal circumstances? And then there is the psychological cunning of the extreme cases: how can I force a woman to carry in her womb and bring to term a child produced by rape? Consider analogous arguments applied to robbery or murder and we can immediately see all of its weaknesses. A very efficacious technique that is now being used in the campaign in favor of euthanasia: I would never kill myself, but in the face of pain without end, why must I prevent others from ending their suffering? I would never kill my child, but in the face of a life dragged on without hope how can I prevent a father from ... ? And in almost every case there are innocents forced to suffer the sinful choices of others: the child in an abortion, the sick person in the case of euthanasia, children in the case of families that fall apart.*

Growing Up: A Right That Has Been Violated

"Let the children come to me, do not hinder them; for to such belongs the kingdom of God" (Mark 10:14). Immediately after this, in all three synoptic Gospels, the episode of the rich young man is narrated, the one whom Jesus loved and whom He asked to leave everything and follow Him. He indicates in children the path to perfection. He asks the young to follow Him with the same simplicity as they had in their infancy. In five of the last six great apparitions recognized by the Church, Our Lady appeared to children and adolescents: La Salette, Lourdes, Fátima, Banneux, and Kibeho. In the fifth, at Rue du Bac in Paris, she appeared to a young nun who tells that she was guided in the dark of night to her first encounter with the Virgin Mary by her guardian angel who appeared to her in the form of a child. The visionaries in Medjugorje were all young children when the first apparitions took place.

"Let the children come to me, do not hinder them." An exhortation and a command that have been systematically disregarded. The family and society have not helped children to come near to Jesus, just as they have not assisted adolescents and young adults in choosing to follow him. In both cases, they often impeded them. *From this point of view, it is easy to understand how it is that youth are the easy prey of evil and, in a certain sense, are preferred victims. Because they are inexperienced, simple, ill-equipped, easily taken advantage of, and excited. They do not pray, because no one has taught them to do so or shown them the extraordinary richness and serenity that come from prayer. When they do pray, they often give up quite early. Distance from God is for them the main reason why they are at risk. They set sail on the sea of life like skiffs without a rudder. The second risk comes from not recognizing any laws from above. In this way they burn on a bonfire without end, without having understood all the wonderful things life has offered them, beginning with love and sex. The third risk is found in the occasions of life, the company they keep, mass media. Then there are the satanic cults and rock music, spiritualistic seductions, rave parties, alcohol, and the use of drugs.*

All this is taken lightly, as a necessary experience, which then embroils them, and from which they cannot get out. Among the occasions of life there are the problems, the real ones, like unemployment. For young people it is a serious affliction that derails them. Many who have graduated and have degrees still cannot find a job. And as we know, idleness is the father of vices. Even more tremendous, especially for adolescents and twenty-somethings, is the great deceit of immortality. It is easy for youth to think death cannot touch them. Thus, if they cannot give meaning to their lives, death is a distant reality to them, which they can easily challenge. Youth arouse such compassion in me. They do not have ideals they can believe in. They absorb vices with extreme facility. I have seen in them the immense harm done by games, and by sex without rules, without love. We must teach them the meaning of life. What does a man gain by winning the world if he loses his soul?

In the book *Youth and Esoterism*, the author Carlo Climati takes his cue from a provocative phrase by Don Orione: "Youth are the either the tempest or the sunshine of the future." This is the synthesis of the educational problem. The future of society depends on what one is able to teach youth today. *But what does mass media teach youth? Reality TV shows come to mind, or the easy money they promise; it is such poor education, because they distract youth from serious, realistic, and qualifying work commitments and efforts. I so often tell parents:*

in Baptism you accepted the responsibility of giving a Christian education to your children, but to their souls you have paid no attention, or you teach them the paths to Hell.

Youth have an innate sense of generosity, a spirit of helping their neighbor. One sees it during terrible calamities, in cases of extreme need. In ordinary life, however, if we do not propose a true ideal to them, they risk surrendering themselves to the fashions and interests of those who want to exploit their naïveté. The first example that comes to mind is that of music, especially a certain type of rock music that is explicitly satanic or was written or performed by people dedicated to the occult, to spiritualistic rites, or to outright satanism.

Many examples can be cited naturally which fall outside of technical considerations of the music. By its nature, a good part of rock music is, so to speak, an invitation to moral disengagement. Behind the great musical gathering of Woodstock in 1969, which hid behind the pacifist ideology of the flower children with the slogan "Peace, love, and music," was the same desecrating and transgressive logic of modern raves. In fact, the word "rave" simply means "delirium." And that a certain type of music seeks to lead us to delirium can be comprehended by the rhythmic use of bass notes in an increasingly insistent, alienating, dehumanizing way, as in the tribal initiation dances, or the propitiatory ones of shamans. The fact is, that in these situations, every type of inhibition to one's sexual drives disappears, making widespread use of alcohol and various intoxicating substances, and risking one's life in wild car races, is only a consequence. The fact that groups of youth identify themselves increasingly with tribal habits and symbolism (the language of gestures, piercing, tattoos), even when they meet each other online or on the phone, simply confirms the frequent and perhaps myopic habit of some sociologists and musicians of explaining youth phenomena in tribal terms.

A case apart is esoteric or satanic rock, the type that is inspired by and makes direct reference to the devil, and which is driven by the ethos "Do what thou wilt shall be the whole of the law," which was the favorite slogan of the English occult leader Aleister Crowley. He is considered the founder of modern occultism, according to which "there is no other god but man and man has the right to live according to his own laws."

Do What Thou Wilt

The desire to astound and attract youth has from the beginning pushed many rock musicians to insert into their lyrics or their album covers esoteric and moral references drawn from the logic of man as the sole god. It is said that among the first to suffer this influence were the Beatles who, among the many faces that inhabit the album cover of *Sgt. Pepper's Lonely Hearts Club Band,* included that of Crowley. "We wanted to gather together the faces of the people we love and admire," explained their drummer Ringo Starr in an interview. The Beatles did not participate in the occult. They were nonetheless among the first to refer to drug use.

Among Crowley's followers is Anton LaVey, who founded the Church of Satan, of which Marilyn Manson, the king of diabolic rock, is a priest. We know with certainty that the members of a satanic cult of youth were among his fans, a cult which came into the headlines sadly some years ago, when two of their members killed a nun in Val Chiavenna, high in the Italian Alps. Their diaries were full of satanic symbols, invocations to Satan constructed in the same way as normal invocations to Christ and the Virgin Mary, and phrases attributed to their favorite singer such as, "Kill your mom and dad and, in an act of hopeless rock and roll behavior, kill yourself."

There are also cases of kids who have committed suicide for no apparent reason. News reports told the world of an episode that happened in a small town in Apulia in the spring of 2002: "In the boy's room, the police officers found dozens of CDs of the cursed singer, and his walls were covered with posters of the rock star exalting death." Obsessed with Manson's music was another boy from Sesto San Giovanni, who in that same period stabbed to death his girlfriend at school. At the time, some wanted to denounce the singer for the plagiarism found in his lyrics. One notes that Manson's pseudonym, although making reference to Marilyn Monroe, was inspired by the actions of the killer Charles Manson, famous for having openly identified himself as a follower of Satan and founding a cult responsible for various homicides. The above-quoted "Do what thou wilt shall be the whole of the law" appears on an album by Led Zepplin, whose guitarist, Jimmy Page, has never hidden his affection for Crowley, to the point of buying his former country house on the shores of Loch Ness.

The arrival of heavy metal increased the already frequent satanic references, both on album covers as well as in lyrics, where one speaks of pacts with the devil, satanic rites, and human sacrifice. They make common usage of symbols like the upside-down cross, the pentagram, and the number of the beast. Many album covers are simply bad taste. On one cover by the group Törr, there appears a crucified Christ who is decomposing. In another by Deliverance, there is a photograph of a little girl with the words "Devil's Meat" written on her forehead. On one album by Celtic Frost, Christ on the Cross is used as a slingshot. Sadly, the invitation to suicide inserted into one of Ozzy Osbourne's songs is widely known. A record by Megadeath makes reference to euthanasia.

On the records of some groups, among them Queen and Led Zepplin, there are satanic messages cut into them, audible only when played backward, the practice of backmasking. When listening in the proper way they are inaudible, but one must ask why they are there in the first place, hidden in reverse, as are all Satan's works. Consider the example of a song by the band Enigma: When played forward, one hears a Gregorian chant in Latin that sings the praises of purity and faith in Christ with angels and children. When played in reverse, one hears the panting of a couple having sex.

What is peculiar is the fact that the inspiring principle of the esoteric and satanic thread that runs from Crowley to LaVey and Manson succeeds in denying the existence of the devil, placing oneself at the center of adoration, a perfect fusion of the logic of twentieth-century nihilism and contemporary hedonism. Furthermore, in Friedrich Nietzsche's famous *Thus Spoke Zarathustra,* he exalts as a noble virtue "the egoism that flows from a soul thirsting for power," juxtaposed with every form of Christian virtue, because "the one who refuses to defend himself is hateful, contemptible, contemptible the one who swallows the spit and tolerates the evil glances, the one who is too patient, too resigned, too satisfied: all that is servile. . . . And one who is servile before the gods and the divine, or to men and foolish human opinion, is the same thing: blessed egoism spits on every servile custom."

In open harmony with this logic is the use of tattoos and piercing, which take to extremes the cult of the body and the full sovereignty of man over it, arriving at brutalizing it with indelible images, to the point of obliterating every human feature.

Unlike rock music, tattoos and piercing are not necessarily done with evil intentions. They do not necessarily have evil meanings. As such, the fact that a person wants to decorate his body with rings or patterns is nothing to be condemned. One must look at the motives, why they are doing these things, the symbolism used, the philosophy, and the eventual rites that are behind them. It is important to establish these things. There are tattoos or piercings that have precise aims, that signify belonging, or one's that are done for sexual reasons, because one hates ones own body or life in general, or because one wants to show the devil one's allegiance to him. In many cases, they are simply actions that do not decorate but rather dishonor the body and that, as negative as they might be, do not arise from any particular malice. It must be noted, nevertheless, that there are books that connect so-called body art to various forms of the occult and the esoteric, making broad use of declarations and interviews of the founders of satanic cults such as LaVey and other followers of Crowley.

Another problem is that of comic books, cartoons, and picture cards. *There are those who are hunting children. There are some horrible comic books. Quite often, they spread the mania for the horrid. They do not display any sense of the beautiful. They are occult carriers of magic, satanism, and insolence. Parents must be very careful when they buy comics for their children, careful about what types of cartoons they watch. In many cases they are trying to corrupt children through these images and stories. Of course, we should not generalize, and there are exceptions to be made. But there is no doubt, for example, that many animes and mangas propound a vision of the world in perfect harmony with esotericism and magic. They are often rich in images and effects that closely recall the devil in his various common iconographical usages, without necessarily identifying him as an evil that should be avoided. Also, many films for youth and adolescents insinuate a negative vision of the world, and distance their viewers from the truth, introducing them to magic and an esoteric vision of existence. Not to mention horror films and certain series in which malevolence is never defeated but always rises up once more, suggesting the perverse principle that it is always evil and not good that triumphs. In this regard, there is an interesting volume by Annalisa Colzi,* How Satan Corrupts Society, *that should be essential reading for those wanting to understand the devil's particular interest in youth through using the media.*

And when one speaks of young people, one cannot help but think of the weekly slaughter in automobile accidents. *In these situations, one can easily see the devil's work of tempting and inspiring. The very fact that there is such a high toll of serious injuries and loss of life, especially among youth, makes it clear how in this matter the work of the devil can be seen. The devil urges people to perform dangerous actions and sports with the intention of taking their lives. The carelessness of young people often makes them easy prey to the worst temptations—those, to be clear, on a path of no return. We cannot repeat enough that alcohol and limitless pleasure seeking, the use of intoxicating substances, the euphoria of speed, the sensation of immortality, the lack of respect for life and the safety of others, the violation of laws, and depersonalizing the individual through exhausting musical rhythms are all pieces in a puzzle in which it is easy to identify the work of the devil.*

One might also ask why car makers are not obliged to build cars that cannot exceed the speed limit, given that in the end, there would be no ill effect on the market, because the status symbol regarding the car could be easily transferred to other accessories justifying luxury and super luxury. And why then is it so easy and socially acceptable to violate the speed limit and all the safety norms of the rules of the road?

Such things might take us far from our topic or perhaps too near to the question of the influence of evil in society. *The fact remains that the devil is never far from all that provokes and can provoke death. I have witnessed road accidents in which the devil acted directly. These are fairly common cases that lead one to think of curses and spells. I remember in particular an accident that happened to people I had been accompanying, in which the cars were totally destroyed but those inside were miraculously unscathed. I was able to verify the direct evil influence that provoked the accident as well as the divine protection of those in the cars. On one side the curse, on the other the superior power of divine protection. I have also had cases in which I learned of specific curses such as, "You'll die in a car crash." Many of the people who have come to me for exorcisms have had accidents of this type without suffering any physical harm.*

Finally, we cannot overlook the Internet and new electronic media. These issues merit an analysis of the positive and the negative they have done. We add nothing to what is already known in recalling that one can find online guides for experiencing direct encounters with the demonic, expressly addressing youth. There is no lack of aberrations. There are even websites where one can pay for the production of videos that show in detail the perverse, homicidal fantasies of the customer.

But perhaps it is not in these settings that the true "diabolical" power of electronic communications should be sought. *The greatest problem is the fact that they isolate people.* Upon reflection, we are witnessing a proliferation of solitary games and entertainment that allow for the construction of one's own virtual world that can do without external contact. At the same time, all the most fashionable systems of mass entertainment or pastimes do not facilitate interpersonal communication, but rather render it more difficult. Dance clubs as well as raves and social networks are enlightening examples. *Perhaps the moment has come to consider a new pedagogy of entertainment, to return to teaching the reasons for communication and beauty.*

On Avarice, Sex, and Other Deviations

WHERE THERE IS EVIL there is always the suggestion of the devil. What most interests him is to have man fall into sin. He supplies the temptations. He seeks our weak spot and our predisposition. He tries to substitute God with idols inspired by our great passions: pride, riches, and pleasure. He invites each of us to construct his own idol according to our specific tendencies: success, power, ambition, bullying, violence, money, acquisitiveness, sex, drugs, gluttony, gambling.

St. Paul writes that greed for money is the root of all evils. In one of his fioretti, St. Francis told of having seen the devil outside the walls of the monastery shoveling a pile of something into the monastery. As he approached to see better what it was, he realized that the pile consisted of gold coins. The devil was hurling them into the monastery to corrupt the friars' vow of poverty. It was said of John XXIII that before becoming pope, he would often reprimand religious communities and individual religious for their infidelity to their vow of poverty. Visiting an important Franciscan monastery once, he saw a great marble staircase quite refined and precious. He asked the meaning of such ostentation in a place of poverty. Their response was, "Holy Father, thanks to the vow of poverty, we place all in common and collect the money which then allows us to do these works."

He then noticed a large sitting room well-furnished, also with a precious marble floor. He asked again for an explanation and received the same answer. He then wittily replied, "I understand. I wonder then how many children you have thanks to your vow of chastity!"

The Gospel admonition comes to mind: "Beware lest you fall into temptation." The cunning of evil has no limits. And there is no doubt that sex is one of the great instruments of temptation in the hands of the devil. Alfonso Maria De Liguori claimed, "One goes to Hell on account of sex, or not without that fault." To Jacinta of Fátima, when she was seven years old and still knew nothing of these matters, they asked her, based on the visions, which sin sends the most souls to Hell. She replied without hesitating: "the impure sin."

St. John of the Cross taught his Carmelites that of all enemies, "the flesh is the most tenacious and its assaults last as long as a man's life." Furthermore, the attention of many saints was not to fall into this type of temptation, as is well known. Famous as well is that the path of sanctity of many of them began precisely with the choice to leave behind a life of lust and vice. It is the sin in which temptation has the easiest time. And the devil seeks in every way to foster such temptations.

The fact that in our society one abuses, often with arrogance, sexual enticements is in some way a confirmation of the existence of the devil. But even more subtle is the systematic abuse of the word love. *The highest Christian value is distorted and manipulated to the point of presenting it in a manner contrary to how Christ proposed it. If in Christ love is the bearer of union and peace, the concept of love proposed by the world produces division, hatred, and war. Love and physical attraction are two distinct things. In a solid couple they stand together in a proper balance, but remain distinct. Husband and wife, who give the right emphasis to both, transform their love into that perfect and lasting union that is the continuation of the divine creative action.*

Families are torn apart over this point. Sex as physical attraction is privileged. Love is reduced to the sense of romantic satisfaction, of that purely personal enjoyment publicized by mass media. One is always on the lookout for new stimulating experiences. The truth is lost sight of, division is sown, and what one believed to be love is quickly transformed into dissatisfaction, enmity, hatred, jealousy, violence: all the fruit of diabolical deception.

It is said that these things are so widespread because we have lost the sense of the family which was once so solid. But for a sense of family to exist it is essential to educate. Recent generations, which no longer see in the family a point of reference where love can grow within it, have been educated according to the concept of love offered by a transgressive culture, which utilizes the media as its essential weapon. All the so-called taboos have fallen as we chase after fantasies and the myth of freedom, which, upon scrutiny, has never come to fruition. Women were supposed to be freer, and men too, without having to maintain their image or the family at all costs. But how can one say, observing the nooses tied by bureaucracy, our consumer economy, and our way of managing children of divorced parents, that there have been gains in freedom and not, instead, greater constraints. Not to mention the harm done to children who then grow up with misplaced expectations of freedom and the risk (in many cases verified) that the cycle starts all over, but this time from an even lower level.

The logic is that which can be seen in the words and behaviors of many personalities that the media canonize as celebrities. A former president of a large South American country, during a convention on "Drugs and Democracy" being held in Rio de Janeiro in August 2009, claimed that "humanity has always taken some type of drug, and to imagine a world without drugs is like imagining a world without sex. Our struggle, then, and our advice is (to use the same metaphor) safe sex, not the abolition of sex. George W. Bush preached that against AIDS it was better to live life without sex. We have always preferred the idea of safe sex."

This reasoning that uses paradox as a metaphor ends up assimilating the concept of sex to that of drugs. It is easy to apply this logic to that which made places like Las Vegas a true factory of consumer marriages, to the point that unions can be celebrated in a "drive-through" fashion. The couple drives up in their car, or in a rented limousine, stops at the window of the civil servant who signs the documents, and they're ready for their honeymoon.

The slogan of Crowley, "Do what thou wilt," returns obsessively. And an analogous discussion can be made for homosexuality. Confusing sexual relations with loving relations, people began to speak of free love, then of a right to love that is valid for everyone, and then the right to live one's own sexuality and one's vices openly, of rights for every type of couple to be a family, to have children, and so forth. Thus, while on one side the right to destroy the heterosexual family is established, on the other they support the right to construct homosexual families founded on couples who, by their very nature, cannot be stable in the construction of the love that is the effect of the divine plan which we spoke of; if anything, these are harbingers of even greater tragedies for their eventual children.

As always, if we raise our belly to the status of a god, it becomes capable of anything. The final taboo in the race of this false "freedom to love" is that of children. Let us hope that society resists this urge. Let us pray it will hold. Today, even pedophilia has become widespread in all levels of society. The painful appeals of the pope against this practice in the Church are a demonstration of this. There are those who use the means of mass communication to spread it, those who exploit their standing to take advantage of children, those who take long trips to violate children in lands far away. There are even those who advocate the liberalization of pedophilia, taking their cue from the open practice of pedophilia in pre-Christian antiquity, showing once more that in all these cases the work of the devil is to distance man, society, and the Church from Jesus Christ and His teachings. It is a true devastation of human dignity, before which there is great need for a renewed Christian commitment.

Always pertinent is one of St. Leo the Great's homilies dedicated to Christmas, titled "Remember, O Christian, Your Dignity." Pope Leo explains that ever since the Lord was born, "there has been no room for sadness," because "a life which destroys death and gives the joy of the eternal promises" was also born at that time. No one is excluded from this felicity. The cause of joy is common to all because our Lord, the victor over sin and death, has come to liberate all of us. The saint should exult because his reward is near; the sinner should rejoice because forgiveness has been offered to him; the pagan should rediscover his courage because he is now called to life. The Son of God, desiring to reconcile human nature with its Creator, assumed nature Himself in such a way that the devil, the bringer of death, would be vanquished by the same creature whom he had made his slave. ... Recognize, O Christian, your dignity. Made participant in the divine nature, do not return to vileness through unworthy conduct. Remember that, stolen from the powers of darkness, you have been transferred into the light of the Kingdom of God. ... Do not submit yourself once again to the slavery of the devil. Remember that the price paid for your redemption is the Blood of Christ."

Attack on the Divinity of Jesus

What makes the devil proudest? Considering that the sin of pride, or *superbia,* is at the foundation of all human malice, violence, and perversity, the question comes naturally.

I have often asked the devil during exorcisms: "If you could go back in time, what would you have chosen? Would you still choose to reject God?" He has always answered me, "I would make the same choice." And once when I insisted with the same question he even highlighted: "Don't you understand that I had the strength to rebel against God? This means I'm superior to Him."

A limitless pride and arrogance that, translated into actions, is pure malice. It is a malice exercised with the aim of denying the divinity and power of God, despite the fact that he is aware that good is destined to triumph. It is an ostentatious fury that is even paradoxical. His rush to reject God is so great, in fact, that he ends up confirming not only His existence but also His sovereignty over creation.

Can it be said that the devil is one of the proofs of the existence of God? *We can not only say that, but that is truly the case! In his manifestations, the devil confirms the whole of salvation history. His terror of Jesus Christ, of the Virgin Mary, and of all that is sacred is obvious and real. It is also evident that satanists believe blindly in the real presence of Christ in the consecrated bread and wine. They believe in this and for this reason dedicate their lives to profaning it: profaning Jesus to exalt the ephemeral power of the devil. Like the devil, they want to be profoundly evil, black inside, to hold hostage the infinite goodness of Jesus, the pure love of Mary, and their work of redemption of souls. It becomes obvious, then, that those who risk their lives dedicating themselves to works of evil are not acting in freedom as they would like to believe, but as slaves in the devil's struggle against God. A struggle he is destined to lose. Those who commit their lives to evil are fighting under the wrong banner, and have lost before it ever began.*

The first chapter of the Letter to the Romans is explicit on this point. While on one hand, Paul emphasizes that "He who through faith is righteous shall live" (v. 17), on the other he defines as "without excuse" those who "although they knew God they did not honor him as God or give thanks to him, but they became futile in their thinking and their senseless minds were darkened" (v. 21). Because "claiming to be wise, they became fools, and exchanged the glory of the immortal God for images resembling mortal man or birds or animals or reptiles. Therefore God gave them up in the lusts of their hearts to impurity, to the dishonoring of their bodies among themselves, because they exchanged the truth about God for a lie and worshipped and served the creature rather than the Creator. … For this reason God gave them up to dishonorable passions … and receiving in their own persons the due penalty for their error. And since they did not see fit to acknowledge God, God gave them up to a base mind and to improper conduct. Though they know God's decree that those who do such things deserve to die, they not only do them but approve those who practice them" (vv. 22–32).

These words are extremely pertinent to our times. Upon close scrutiny, they recall the meaning of Hell. Forgetfulness of God brings with it the worst of moral and social disorders. "For this reason God gave them up," recalls St. Paul repeatedly, as if to say that sin, not recognized as such through repentance, bears its own condemnation. The reference to the sixth chapter of Genesis concerning the flood is direct: "The Lord saw that the wickedness of man was great in the earth, and that every imagination of the thoughts of his heart was only evil continually" (v. 5).

This is the work of the devil: to redirect attention from God to earthly things; to deny the saving action of Jesus, deriding the promise of eternal happiness, insisting on that which is considered the only liberation, that can only come through giving free rein to one's senses. And we do well, at a certain point in life, to recognize that we have been chasing after nothing, that we have wasted our entire existence for a fistful of dust.

A character in one of Gabriel D'Annunzio's works comes readily to mind, perhaps as an image of the author himself. In *Pleasure*, one finds precisely this sense of nothingness unleashed by a dissolute life. His problem is not with his sense of guilt, but that the feeling of being free to sin that he had so longed for in reality ended up binding him like "a fastened chain." The sentiment he feels is "the immense sadness of loves that have become tired habits," as well as the distress in noticing that "his inert hands" can no longer grasp "the lacerated veil of illusions." It is sin that accompanies him to his condemnation, the great biblical deluge that falls on the heart of the man who has rejected God and has been "abandoned to the caprice of his depraved intelligence." This is the desperation of Faust, the defeat of a life. St. Thomas Aquinas wrote, "Intemperance is most disgusted by nobility and decency, for in the pleasures concerning intemperance the light of reason is often obfuscated, that light from which all the nobility and beauty of virtue are derived."

Is this like saying the devil makes pots but not the lids? *It sounds flippant but it is very much the case. Consider the enormous effort he went to first to tempt Jesus then to eliminate him. Limitless effort and malice. After having seen the film* The Passion of the Christ, *although it seemed to many to have dwelt too much on the demonic sufferings of the Redeemer, John Paul II, already quite tested by pain and sickness, commented: "That is exactly how it was." To carry out his purpose of having Him killed by the men whom Christ had come to save from his dominion, the devil corrupted Judas, the Sanhedrin, Herod, Pilate, and the crowd that asked for Barabbas. He did so in a way that Jesus would be judged in the most unjust trial in history. He urged Pilate to have Him scourged to placate the wrath of the people. He pushed the soldiers to unload on Him their repressed anger and even to crown Him with thorns. He did everything possible so that He would be crucified in the most atrocious and humiliating way possible. In the end, however, the death of Christ was revealed to be the devil's defeat.*

There is an attempt to completely humanize Jesus, to place in doubt His divinity and, vice versa, to divinize Him completely so as to place in doubt His death and consequently His Resurrection, an attempt which has continued for centuries. Many heresies have arisen for one or the other motive. Entire religions and many cults that call themselves Christian, as well as various movements and cultural currents, have all promoted the immanence of Jesus Christ. Even theological modernism, in more recent times, born of the just resolve to draw faith and science together, ended, in its most exasperated version, with an affirmation of the humanity of Christ that, in fact, denied His transcendence.

There are also those who have attempted in every way to place in dialogue science with magic and the esoteric, exploiting the figure of Jesus, either as a game or as a literary exercise, or even for esoteric, desecrating purposes, if not outright diabolic ones. Typical is their insistence on the supposed love relationship between Jesus and Mary Magdalen. Taking their cue from a painting by Leonardo, they have constructed stories and promoted fantasies that portray Jesus as a magician, as a cultivator of esoteric sciences; anything but God. If Jesus falls in love with a person, in fact, it cannot be the God of the Gospels who loves each person in the same way. The Jesus who loves the Magdalen physically cannot be God. The things that belonged to Him can, however, be magical. From this was born the legend of the Holy Grail that has been handed down for centuries, and which, interestingly, often fuses with the forbidden love for the Magdalen.

The issue concerning the true God and true man is pesky for many, as it is for the devil. A problem that involves issues tied to esoterism, and lodges and associations more or less secret, deviated branches of Freemasonry, magic, and satanic cults.

In this desecration of Christ, exasperated and ideologized secularism, the secularism which the West learned in the age of the Enlightenment, plays a large role. An emblem of this is the attack on public display of the crucifix. In the name of state secularism, civil society must be stripped of any acknowledgment of Christianity. This is the common aim of those without any religious faith and of those who, on the contrary, want to make room for beliefs that deny the divinity of Christ. It is a coincidence of intentions between two positions that are polar opposites and that are in theory irreconcilable, which leads one to intuit a common diabolical inspiration. The defeat suffered by means of the Cross of Christ is, for the devil, an enormous humiliation, and evidence of his own weakness. For this reason, the Cross is heavily contested. It is a destructive campaign that should arouse active resistance in any Christian, as echoed in the words of John Paul II pronounced on June 21, 1998: "Many things can be taken from us Christians. But the cross as a sign of salvation we will not allow them to take. We will not allow it to be excluded from public life."

THE GURU'S CONCOCTION

THERE ARE TWO SOURCES of knowledge for man: a natural one and a supernatural one. Both come from God the Creator, and there can never be contradiction between them. Natural knowledge concerns what is visible, sensible, demonstrable. It includes all that man comes to know through the use of his reason, and therefore through science, technology, exploration, medicine, and so forth. Supernatural knowledge is, on the other hand, a direct consequence of divine revelation.

All peoples, in every time and place, have an idea of evil, of evil spirits that must be ingratiated with rites, sacrifices, often even human sacrifices. Only revelation clarifies that evil, the evil spirits, are demons, in other words, angels that rebelled against God their Creator. Very intelligent beings with great powers. We know from revelation that the soul is immortal, that Paradise, Purgatory, and Hell exist, that there will be a particular judgment and a universal judgment, and so forth. All these are elements through which we have been given the ability to comprehend the meaning, value, and purpose of our existence. We know these truths only because God has revealed them to us. We could never have gained scientific knowledge of them. If one believes in revelation, one believes in these truths. This life has meaning only as a stage in a journey toward the truth. For this reason, the study of Scripture is important, because it is the revealed Word which one can either believe or not believe.

In this sense, only Christianity supplies the exact explanation of the nature of evil. In creation, everything came from God. Then came the rebellion of Lucifer and his angels. Then man, when tempted, accepted the devil's offer and caused the wound of Original Sin, which made doing the good much more difficult for him than doing evil. From that day on, to pursue the good one must fight with the devil and one's personal inclinations, and form a strong character in friendship with God. All other religions give different explanations, save Judaism, which is founded on the same revelation, although it does not recognize in Jesus the Messiah announced throughout the Old Testament.

The entire story of Israel is a history of the battle between fidelity to God and rebellion against God. It is a history of betrayal and return, of great actions of faith and of atrocities. At the time, every locality had its own idols. And so, in its wanderings, the chosen people were constantly tempted by idolatry. Every time they had to choose. The discourse of Joshua before the tribes of Israel gathered in Shechem is typical. After having summarized the history of the chosen people, he placed an ultimate choice before everyone: "Now therefore fear the Lord, and serve him in sincerity and in faithfulness; put away the gods which your fathers served beyond the River, and in Egypt, and serve the Lord. And if you be unwilling to serve the Lord, choose this day whom you will serve, whether the gods your father served in the region beyond the River, or the gods of the Amorites in whose land you dwell; but as for me and my house, we will serve the Lord" (Jos. 24:14–15).

Evil has always been present, but the explanations given for this reality have been entirely human and partial with respect to those given by revelation, even though God is Father of all and even though there exist seeds of truth in all the great religions. Consequently, for non-Christian religions and non-revealed religions, their defenses against evil are fewer. In those settings, evil acts more powerfully. In the entire non-Christian world, Satan's actions are even stronger, even though the followers of those religions are not aware of this and cannot entirely comprehend the cunning of the devil. The reality is that demons are all trying to drag us down to Hell.

As concerns the new religions, those who believe in revelation cannot deny that they are all human inventions. Generally speaking, they are not demonic, even though there is no doubt that the devil has no problem interfering there as well. The New Age movement is the maximum expression of the agglomeration of all the possible errors one can imagine. Dante would say that it could not hold water "for the contradiction it does not allow." So many people believe in reincarnation because they have not the least sense of the Resurrection of Christ. It is a pious human desire. I think in some cases there is in this a positive aspect. Although in an erroneous manner, those who believe in reincarnation desire the immortality of their soul, and understand that everything cannot end in this brief earthly sojourn.

All Eastern religions are based on reincarnation. Sai Baba, to give an example, even predicted his future reincarnation, and thanks to belief in reincarnation, he attracts a lot of people. There are many in the affluent West who go to him in the hope of finding a spirituality that satisfies them. Thanks to their donations, Sai Baba has accumulated great economic power and is able to carry out charitable works throughout the world, which reinforce his charisma. The Christian must not forget what St. Paul says to the Ephesians, that we must "speak the truth in love," tending through this "toward Christ," with the aim of no longer being "children, tossed to and fro and carried about with every wind of doctrine, by the cunning of men, by their craftiness in deceitful wiles." Truth in love and, as Benedict XVI emphasizes in the encyclical of the same name, "Charity in truth," because "only in truth does charity shine and can it be authentically lived. Truth is the light that gives meaning and value to charity," otherwise "love becomes an empty shell to be arbitrarily filled,... an abused and distorted word to the point at which it assumes an opposite meaning."

And yet many people who have been to Sai Baba have come to me to convince me of the goodness of his actions. To reinforce their view, they told me that he speaks well of everyone, even of Jesus and the Virgin Mary. The problem is that he considers himself a god. In my opinion, the devil is at work in these cases. All the elements are there that lead us to maintain this. Many of these gurus make powders that can heal every illness. They offer them to their followers, who then often come to me and to other exorcists for help because of the many problems those potions have caused. And from my experience, it is always very difficult to liberate them. One of these people had a true demonic possession. Others were only under the influence of evil. I have had many cases of people who were looking for easy mystical experiences in esoteric settings and places but instead wound up encountering the devil.

Every so often, we are confronted in the news with the experiences of people who have encountered the devil and did not survive to tell the story. Some of these have even been documented in court records. One such case, for example, involved two boys who disappeared in the summer of 2006 in the tropical jungles of South America. Six other Italians, who were traveling with them to participate in shamanic rites involving the use of ayahuasca, are under investigation. The bodies of the two were cut to pieces by a chainsaw and found closed in bags, along with thirteen other cadavers. The story is still shrouded in mystery, but seems linked to magical rites practiced by a local tribe that makes money from trafficking human organs and from selling shrunken heads, as well as from the participation in their rites by Westerners looking for extreme experiences.

It is difficult not to see the hand of Satan in all this human malice. And one wonders how people can plan and embark on journeys that have as their only purpose witnessing or actively participating in such actions. Without going into the details of such obvious brutality, one wonders how people can jump into the dangers of mystical experiences sold by gurus, shamans, and magicians of every sort. *But we also need to ask ourselves why it is that we Catholics are no longer able to offer a strong witness, one that represents a real alternative. And not only in the West. The statistics are frightening, for example, in Latin America, where every year tens of thousands of Catholics abandon the Church and enter cults. They are often of Christian inspiration, even though they propound a Jesus Christ very different from the one found in the Gospels, and at other times these cults are new religions in the strict sense, like Scientology, or voodoo, or Santería, and so forth. In the West, people abandon Christianity to follow vague syncretic philosophies, Islam, Eastern religions, and gurus of every type. Now, for people without religion or born in those cultures, it is entirely comprehensible. The drama is when those who know Jesus Christ, our one Master, abandon Him to follow other beliefs.*

All this demonstrates a deficit in the propagation of the Faith and a frightening religious ignorance. Why look for answers elsewhere to the questions one has when one can easily find them in Christ? Why is the average proposition of Faith that comes out of our parishes that of a child's Christianity? There is no need to go begging among other religions to learn to develop better one's own interiority. And one cannot be a Christian while following New Age practices or the advice of a pseudo-oriental guru, because these things are from the evil one.

How can we defend ourselves from this culture that advocates ethical relativism and a melting pot of religions? *The indispensable remedies can be reduced to three items: a new religious instruction, understood in cultural terms and in spiritual terms, a new evangelization — exact and objective information from a Catholic point of view on what the sects are in all their various forms, whether other religions or New Age cults — and above all, listening to the individual, to his problems and aspirations, to be able to bring back the splendor of love in him, of mercy, of light in the welcome of Christ, the awareness that only in Him, as St. Peter says, are "words of eternal life" to be found. Only in this way can we hope that more and more people can reasonably avoid giving in to the fascination of the stories of friends who have encountered gurus or practiced meditation and are enthusiastic to the point of elation.*

The fourth chapter of the First Letter of St. John comes to our aid: "Do not believe every spirit, but test the spirits to see whether they are of God; for many false prophets have gone out into the world. By this you know the spirit of God: every spirit which confesses that Jesus Christ has come in the flesh is of God, and every spirit which does not confess Jesus is not of God. This is the spirit of antichrist, of which you heard that it was coming, and now it is in the world already. Little children, you are of God, and have overcome them; for he who is in you is greater than he who is in the world. They are of the world, therefore what they say is of the world, and the world listens to them. We are of God. Whoever knows God listens to us, and he who is not of God does not listen to us. By this we know the spirit of truth and the spirit of error" (vv. 1–6).

An Unwitting Society

"Blessed are those who mourn, for they shall be comforted." This is the Second Beatitude. This consolation is not addressed to those without trust, to those without hope, to those incapable of finding a purpose for their lives. On the contrary, it addresses those who have found hope and purpose on the paths of the Lord, and acting upon this, continue to clash against a hostile world.

In his 2007 book, *Jesus of Nazareth,* Pope Benedict XVI dwells on this concept in particular. The mourning and affliction of which the Lord is speaking, the pope explains, "is non-conformity with evil, is a way of opposing that which everyone is doing and which they impose on the individual as the model for behaving. The world cannot bear this type of resistance and demands participation. This affliction seems to them a denouncement in contrast with the dazed conscience. And that it is. For this reason, the afflicted become the persecuted for righteousness sake." And it is to the afflicted, remarks the pope, that consolation is promised, just as to the persecuted is promised the Kingdom of God, to the poor in spirit, the Kingdom of Heaven. "The Kingdom of God, this is the true consolation: to be under the protection of the power of God and to be sure of His love."

We live in a society that is dazzled by evil. Considering the multiplication of instruments with which one can exercise evil, one might say that our society is subject to evil now more than ever. The West's substantial atheism continues to spread, creating enormous voids and depravations. We are witnessing the progressive de-Christianization of the great Catholic nations, which was one of the warnings Our Lady mentioned in some of her apparitions, beginning in the nineteenth century. In the apparition in Kibeho, in Africa, the Virgin Mary expressly denounced the problems generated by a society without values and without God. We are observing the progressive desertion of the Sunday Mass. To cite an example, in Ireland and Poland, the churches were usually packed, just like in Italy thirty or forty years ago. Speaking with Irish and Polish friends, however, I noticed how Christian sentiment has been progressively decreasing there as well. Among the causes, not the least is the many scandals caused by sexually abusive clergymen.

And not only is the number of practicing Christians decreasing, but also of those who simply call themselves Christians or believers. The clergy is going through a terrible crisis, with the decrease in vocations accompanied by many defections, too often preceded by regrettable conduct. When I was a boy, Italy sent hundreds of missionaries throughout the world. Now, if it were not for the arrival of many non-European priests, many of our parishes would be forced to close.

In this context, the evil one has it easy, even though his actions are openly revealed. This is the fate of the afflicted which Benedict XVI has illustrated for us. A mechanism has been established which almost automatically delegitimizes any reasoning that invites one to reflect on the unhealthy behavior of society. All this in the absence of any awareness on the part of even the most faithful Catholics of the ploys put into action to condition, subjugate, and lead astray their thoughts. Thus, what is good according to mainstream opinion assumes the shape of the politically incorrect, and evil is broadcast as a symbol of the times and of the acquisition of new freedoms, despite the lessons of history that teach that all the worst aspects of the human race have already been abundantly and repeatedly explored.

Emblematic in this sense is the discourse on the action of Satan, given by Paul VI at his audience of November 15, 1972, the entire text of which we shall attach in the appendix. In this discourse, the pope began by asking what the greatest needs of the Church were, and in the first two lines gave this response: "One of the Church's greatest needs is to be defended against the evil we call the Devil."[1] Later, he adds that for the Christian, "Evil is not merely an absence of something but an active force, a living, spiritual being that is perverted and that perverts others. It is a terrible reality, mysterious and frightening. It is a departure from the picture provided by biblical Church teaching to refuse to acknowledge the Devil's existence. . . . He is the hidden enemy who sows errors and misfortunes in human history."

This is an issue, Paul VI regrets, that is "a very important chapter of Catholic doctrine which should be studied again, although it is given little attention today." He then underlines that, although one cannot say that every sin is "directly caused by diabolical action, it is true that those who do not keep watch over themselves with a certain moral rigor are exposed to the influence of the 'mystery of iniquity' cited by St. Paul which raises serious questions about our salvation."

At this point, the pope recalls that the devil "is at work where the denial of God becomes radical, subtle and absurd; where lies become powerful and hypocritical in the face of evident truth; where love is smothered by cold, cruel selfishness; where Christ's name is attacked with conscious, rebellious hatred, where the spirit of the Gospel is watered down and rejected, where despair is affirmed as the last word." Furthermore, he adds, quoting the First Letter of John, "that we are of God, and the whole world is in the power of the evil one."

1 Paul VI, "Confronting the Devil's Power," Eternal Word Television Network, accessed June 30, 2024, https://www.ewtn.com/catholicism/library/confronting-the-devils-power-8986.

Paul VI concludes that this must not lead us to desperation. Our defender is Jesus. "Clothe yourselves in the armor of Christ," as St. Paul advises. Because "the Christian must be a militant." The remedy we read in the Gospel of Mark is "in prayer and fasting." And St. Paul adds, "Be not overcome by evil, but overcome evil with good."

A formidable discourse. It is difficult to find words so well calibrated and efficacious on such a delicate topic. In fact, the defensive reaction of modern and progressive minds was not long in coming. The next day, all the newspapers attacked and, in some ways, derided the pope. How could an intelligent man of great culture like him, a pope of the twentieth century, still entertain superstitions that everyone now relegated to the age of witch hunts?

Such attacks have frequently beleaguered the Church in the past three centuries. We have heard them so many times even in recent years. Today as then, enlightenment is juxtaposed with obscurantism, science with faith, modernity with tradition, and so forth. What follows is the ridiculous, if not tragic, paradox that *the same society that sings the praises of freedom from religious conditioning functions as a loudspeaker of the most peculiar superstitions and spiritual beliefs. From the millenary theories of the day (such as the 2012 Mayan doomsday prophecy), to piquant horoscopes; from red chili peppers worn around the neck or hung on the walls of a home or car, to the coffee grounds; from the success of films and books on the Holy Grail to films about vampires, magicians, wizards, and alchemists; from the growing diffusion of beliefs about the mysterious powers of ancient civilizations to the repeated sightings of UFOs or circles in wheat fields; only to discover that these were all imposters, often devised for the enjoyment of astute pranksters.*

Something quite similar happened around the time of Paul VI's discourse on the action of the devil in society. The same newspapers that tore him to pieces, calling him a medieval holdover, a short time later were united in a sensationalist choir that accompanied the debut in cinemas of the famous film The Exorcist. *And not one of the pope's critics thought of using the same standard in judging the content of that production. In many cases, they even endorsed the film, giving it even greater resonance.*

The Devil in the Gospels

I SHALL NEVER TIRE of recalling that we exorcists are often little tolerant of the clergy, an attitude in obvious contrast with the teaching of the Old and New Testaments. The reasons for this are to be attributed to open doctrinal confusion. Many theologians have denied Jesus' exorcisms. They consider them to be interventions closely connected to the cultural language of the time, adapted to make themselves understood by the people of that period. One of the more popular biblical scholars of the moment wrote a book in which he called into question the two most significant exorcisms narrated in the Gospels, considering them simple healings. According to this well-known biblical scholar, the Gerasene demoniac was only a madman, while the young man at the foot of Mt. Tabor was only an epileptic. And yet, in this second episode, which we shall discuss below, Jesus develops an attentive pedagogy of evangelization.

I think it is due to the formulations of these scholars, unfortunately, that today most of the clergy regards the exorcist as a wizard, the devil as an abstract entity, and diabolical manifestations as downright superstitions. And so, in seminaries and theology departments, with a few exceptions, one gives ever less importance to that part of dogmatic theology which, speaking about God the Creator, considers the angels, their testing, and the rebellion of demons. Even less do they speak about the ordinary action of the devil and about his extraordinary action, which ought to be studied in spiritual theology. In moral theology, the sins against the first commandment are no longer studied — those which go by the name of magic, necromancy, spiritism. These forms of superstition that are stridently fought in the Bible and, as we have seen, have never ceased to be practiced, and today are particularly widespread. And if the devil is no longer mentioned, the result is that he is no longer fought, and one acts as if he did not exist.

There are many bishops who do not nominate an exorcist for their dioceses. But this is an obligation imposed by the Gospel. Benedict XVI indirectly reiterated this in an encounter with exorcists at the end of the general audience of September 14, 2005: "I encourage you to continue in your important ministry in the service of the Church," he told them, and then emphasized the necessity that exorcists be able to work "supported by the vigil attention of bishops," and are followed "by the unceasing prayer of the faithful."

In reality, however, the situation continues to be as we described, one of general indifference. In some European nations, exorcists are almost entirely absent. In Italy there are fewer and fewer. And the people who find themselves disoriented and in ever greater need of assistance do not know to whom they can turn, and are even sent by their priests into the hands of psychologists and psychiatrists who, in these cases, can do nothing.

A charge that can be heard on the lips of any exorcist, with the very same words. One must only ask them. The response of a very busy exorcist, a Carmelite working in the Diocese of Rome, put it well: "Exorcists are literally followed by people looking for an appointment, an interview, a blessing, or who would simply like to be listened to and understood in their torment, in their problem, in their sin. Unfortunately, priests who are dedicated to the mission of listening are fewer and fewer. It is even harder to find priests who think that the problem of the devil is a serious one that must be faced because it bears such suffering. In fact, there are more and more priests who tend to deny or at least underestimate the intervention of the devil in the lives of men. That's why the few exorcists who do this work are literally buried by requests."

For those curious enough to look, just go to a church or a sanctuary where an exorcist receives the faithful with or without an appointment, and you will see how many people are waiting their turn, even just to confess, to hear a word of comfort, some advice, to pray together. In the church where the above-quoted Carmelite works every day, it is easy to get a cross section in just a few hours of the various afflictions and sufferings of the tormented humanity there. And one can immediately see that all social classes and ages are represented there. During a spiritual retreat for exorcists held near Padua on the occasion of St. Anthony's body being displayed, there was an incredible turnout of people seeking help.

Very seldom does one hear a preacher or the priest speak openly about the devil, while instead Jesus spoke continually about him because, as St. Peter mentioned, his presence in our life is "like a roaring lion" and is a problem that concerns everyone. But if a priest has never witnessed an exorcism, how can we expect him to understand the real scope of the problem? If he does not believe in the devil, how can you expect him to face and fight evil for what it is?

These questions were already perfectly illuminated in the first centuries of the Church. To those who believed neither in the existence of the devil nor in the saving power of Jesus Christ, Cyprian offered an invitation in chapter fifteen of his apologetical work *To Demetrianus*: "Come and hear the demons with your own ears, come and see with your own eyes the moment in which, giving way to our exorcisms, to our spiritual scourging and the torture of our prayers, they abandon the bodies of those of whom they had taken possession."

There are many Gospel passages in which the devil is mentioned, in which Jesus invites His followers to cast out demons and heal the sick. The Gospel of Mark in particular, which is the oldest and was written on the eyewitness testimony of those who knew Jesus, from the first verses presents the work of the Savior in close correlation to the tempting and perverting action of the devil. Already in verse 13 of the first chapter, one reads that after being baptized and confirmed by the Father in His earthly mission, Jesus was led by the Spirit into the desert: "And he was in the wilderness forty days, tempted by Satan; and he was with the wild beasts; and the angels ministered to him." The devil arrives at the very start of Jesus' public ministry just as, in the beginning, he tempted the man and the woman in Eden. The evangelist deliberately hastens to emphasize that Jesus lived with wild beasts without suffering any harm, just like Adam before the Fall. This expresses reconciliation with creation, which in Isaiah is announced with reference to the coming of the Messiah: "The wolf shall dwell with the lamb, and the leopard shall lie down with the kid" (11:6).

We should notice that the work of the devil is immediate even in the Gospel of Matthew where, in the second chapter, it is clarified of what the man who refuses the announcement of the Messiah is capable. Herod, who learns of the birth of the king of the Jews from the Wise Men, "was troubled." Even Mary, as the evangelist Luke narrates, "was troubled" at the announcement of the angel. But as opposed to Herod, she accepted within her the Savior in all that this meant in terms of infinite goodness for all humanity. Herod, on the other hand, rejected the Annunciation, and within him grew hatred that led him to commit an atrocious crime: the slaughter of the innocents. Adam and Eve allowed themselves to be tempted by the devil and distanced themselves from God, and their guilt was upon them and on all humanity, as seen in the murderous relationship between their sons. Judas betrayed Jesus, even physically, after the Last Supper, and handed him over to his captors for an easy profit.

The Gospel of Matthew, as distinct from Mark, enters into detail regarding the temptations Jesus underwent in the desert. In the sequence presented in chapter four, in variance with that of Luke, the first temptation concerns food: "If you are the Son of God, command these stones to become loaves of bread" (v. 3). The second concerns pride and power: "If you are the Son of God, throw yourself down; for it is written..." (v. 6). The third concerns wealth and political power: "All these I will give you, if you will fall down and worship me" (v. 9).

"The core of every temptation appears clearly here," Benedict XVI mentions in one of his writings, "to remove God, who in the face of everything in our life that seems more urgent, seems secondary, if not superfluous and bothersome. ... The devil does not invite us directly to commit evil. That would be too crude. He acts as if he is pointing to something better: in the end, to abandon illusions and put our energies to better use in the world. He presents himself under the guise of true realism. The real is what can be verified: power and bread. Compared to this, the things of God appear unreal, a secondary world of which we have no need." In essence, through his cunning, the devil wants to challenge God Himself, His reality, His goodness, or to put it better, the intelligence of our choice in favor of Him. He insinuates doubt about whether we are following the least convenient route, the most illogical. The question he asks us, quoting again from Pope Benedict, is, "Is God good, or must we establish what is good for ourselves?" This is none other than the doubt instilled by the serpent in the minds of Adam and Eve.

It is a doubt instilled daily and successfully in our society, where God has vanished for all intents and purposes and is even chased out of images; where religious traditions are considered bigoted habits, at times quaint, always useless; where the only usefulness granted to religion is political, with the aim of managing and controlling the world. In the face of all this, Benedict XVI states that Jesus comes forth triumphant because, "to the deceitful divinization of power and well-being, to the deceitful promise of a future that guarantees all and everything by means of power and the economy, He has posited the divine nature of God: God as the true good of man."

This is a battle from which man must not flee. *And Jesus shows us the sure path: that of His victory over evil.* We recalled this previously through the words of St. Francis: "Where the fear of God guards the entrance, there the enemy cannot find a way in." Advice, certainty, and great consolation.

"You Have Come to Destroy Us"

From the beginning, then, the Gospels show how accepting Jesus unleashes good, just as evil is unleashed from rejecting Him. Satan plays the omnipresent role of the tempter, the one who seeks to distance us from God and, through man, generate evil on earth.

According to this logic, the reason is entirely clear why in the Gospel of Mark Jesus' first miracle is an exorcism, the healing of a demoniac — in other words, the immediate demonstration of His power over evil. Equally clear is the reason why the episode takes place within a place of worship, almost as if to underline the sharp juxtaposition between God and Satan, between good and evil, between Heaven and Hell.

Jesus "entered the synagogue and taught. And they were astonished at his teaching, for he taught them as one who had authority, and not as the scribes. And immediately there was in their synagogue a man with an unclean spirit; and he cried out, 'What have you to do with us, Jesus of Nazareth? Have you come to destroy us? I know who you are, the Holy One of God.' But Jesus rebuked him, saying, 'Be silent, and come out of him!' And the unclean spirit, convulsing him and crying with a loud voice, came out of him. And they were all amazed, so that they questioned among themselves, saying, 'What is this? A new teaching! With authority he commands even the unclean spirits and they obey him'" (Mark 1:21–27).

There are two things to be distinguished in close connection between them: the astonishment of the people, because the words of Jesus are so different from those usually pronounced by the clergy of the time; and the fear of the people in the face of the manifestation of power over the unclean spirit. This correlation indicates how in Mark the miracle over demons shows concretely the superior authority of Jesus' words. The people observing this put the two together and are amazed. So often, Jesus repeats in the Gospel: if you do not believe my words, at least believe my works, the miracles I have done before your eyes.

His power over demons gives value to the originality and salvific power of the Word. It gives credit to Jesus' teaching, just as later the miracle for the paralytic who is lowered from the roof is used to emphasize and render tangible His power to remit sins. This is a concept that is made explicit in the First Letter of John, which says that Jesus has come to destroy the works of Satan.

Another significant element is that the unclean spirit knows who Jesus is. Paradoxically, it renders Him explicit public witness. This is the first time in the Gospel of Mark that Jesus is introduced to the people for who He really is, after the voice of God heard from Heaven at the moment of His baptism in the Jordan, "Thou art my beloved Son, with thee I am well pleased." Jesus, however, refuses the witness of the demon. He does not want it because it is always contrary to God's plans. It pursues different aims.

The devil wants to validate the natural aspirations of the people who are expecting a warrior Messiah, a powerful king who will defeat the Romans and give power back to the Jewish people. Satan testifies who Jesus is because he wants Him to be glorified by the people, he wants them to put Him on the royal pedestal. Jesus, on the other hand, has him keep silent because that is not His mission: His is to liberate the world from the evil one, and to do so He must suffer and die to be able to rise again. Only in this way is man's true liberation realized.

The exorcism narrated in the Acts of the Apostles is interesting in this regard, the one depicting St. Paul in conflict with the fortune teller who exhorts the people to follow him. St. Paul, like Jesus, commands the devil to keep silent. Paul does not want the publicity, the propaganda, and above all he does not want to be confused with the truth. Paul is not the truth. The truth is the one in whose name the sick are healed and demons are cast out, and thanks to whom one becomes truly free.

The purpose of Jesus, as well as that of St. Paul, is clearly contrary to that of the devil, who wants man to be enslaved and lost. The unclean spirit, as soon as he sees Jesus, reiterates this: "You have come to destroy us." He cannot fail to recognize that Jesus came to destroy the works of Satan, just as we read in the First Letter of John.

The Gerasene Demoniac

The case of the Gerasene Demoniac is different in its context and its narration, which has compelling pedagogical value due to the comprehension of the attitude of the devil with relation to Jesus, as well as the paradoxical attitude of the men to whom it seems entirely normal to reject the good of having been liberated from the obvious harms of the evil one.

"And when he had come out of the boat, there met him out of the tombs a man with an unclean spirit, who lived among the tombs; and no one could bind him any more, even with a chain,... but the chains he wrenched apart, and the fetters he broke in pieces; and no one had the strength to subdue him. Night and day among the tombs and on the mountains he was always crying out and bruising himself with stones" (Mark 5:1–5).

It is striking that the other Gospels narrate that he wandered about naked and was so furious that no one could travel through that area. In Matthew 8, it says that there were two demoniacs. The fact is that Jesus was in the presence of a very dangerous man, harming himself and others. Despite this, he threw himself at the feet of Christ.

"And when he saw Jesus from afar, he ran and worshipped him; and crying out with a loud voice, he said, 'What have you to do with me, Jesus, Son of the Most High God? I adjure you by God, do not torment me.' For he had said to him, 'Come out of the man, you unclean spirit!' And Jesus asked him, 'What is your name?' He replied, 'My name is Legion; for we are many.' And he begged him eagerly not to send them out into the country." There was nearby a herd of swine pasturing and the demons asked Jesus to send them "to the swine, let us enter them." Leaving the man, they entered the pigs, and the entire herd killed itself by stampeding off a cliff into the lake.

The first thing we note is that the devil immediately recognizes who he is dealing with. With respect to the demoniac of the previous narrative, this one defines even better the identity of Jesus: first He was the "Holy One of God," now He is "Son of the Most High God." One wonders at the fact that it would take three years of preaching after these events before Peter was able to affirm the very same things in Caesarea Philippi. And even the apostles always had in mind the Messiah as a political figure. Even after the Resurrection, they were not able to get beyond this. At that point, the response and subsequent courage needed were entrusted to the work of the Holy Spirit.

Here too, Jesus does not want to give space to the witness the devil renders Him, since it was not for the glory of God but to deceive men. He does not allow him to speak, and goads him with His questions. As soon as the devil sees Jesus, moreover, he knows his fate is sealed. He recognizes his defeat and understands that he could no longer remain in the body of the man he was tormenting. The preventive request not to be tormented assumes the dimensions of the excusatio non petita. *In the presence of Jesus, the devil loses his appeal, and is revealed for what he is.*

The questions Jesus asks the devil are a fundamental moment in every exorcism. We pose them following an exact ritual that draws its logic and power precisely from this Gospel passage. We have seen how it is a necessary operation for understanding who we are dealing with and how to perform the exorcism. The devil's response is interesting. He does not tell Him the name, but the number. "My name is legion," which means "there are many of us." (A Roman legion consisted of three hundred soldiers.) *I have met many people possessed by a large number of demons. The purpose of gathering in such numbers is to render the curse even stronger and the liberation more difficult. I am currently following a most serious case of possession in which every time I ask how many of them there are, the answer is always, "We are legion, legion, legion."*

I remember a girl who had a hundred fifty demons. Then after a few exorcisms the number went down to twenty-nine. The following time there were twenty-two. Naturally, the leader was always there, He is the one who organizes all the others. In such cases, they always come out screaming and tortured. Often, when they feel they are forced to leave, they ask the help of other demons. They make distinct cries for help. During exorcisms, however, this request for help is never satisfied. Once forced to leave, the devil must do so without obtaining the help he sought.

In his dialogue with Jesus, the demon asks to remain in the region. Jesus seems to grant him this request. He is pleading that the legion might pass into the herd of swine they see on the hillside nearby. Some two thousand swine are mentioned. In any case, it is an excessive number. Some biblical scholars have suggested that the phrase might be better translated as two herds of swine. Nevertheless, a very large quantity is involved. The fact is, the demons leave the man's body ranting and raving and enter the pigs that run down and throw themselves into the lake, as if they were crazed. This gesture highlights the true aim of the devil: he always seeks destruction and death. The swine, who have no ability to oppose the diabolical influence, immediately commit suicide. The instigation to commit suicide is one of the devil's classic temptations. Jesus liberates the man and allows the devil to free his death-seeking desire on the swine, animals which the Jews consider unclean by nature. All these clear signs are not understood, however.

The inhabitants of that region, in fact, are amazed, but fail to understand. The Gospel continues, "And the people came to see what it was that had happened. And they came to Jesus, and saw the demoniac sitting there, clothed and in his right mind, the man who had had the legion; and they were afraid. And those who had seen it told others what had happened to the demoniac and to the swine. And they began to beg Jesus to depart from their neighborhood. And as he was getting into the boat, the man who had been possessed with demons begged him that he might stay with him. But he refused and said to him. 'Go home to your friends, and tell them how much the Lord has done for you, and how he has had mercy on you.' And he went away and began to proclaim in the Decapolis how much Jesus had done for him; and all men marveled."

The attitude of these people is emblematic of how people often behave with those who have done them some good deed: a mixture of ingratitude and fear of being involved. They were afraid of the demoniac, but now they saw him perfectly calm, serene, no longer naked but dressed. Instead of comprehending the extraordinary nature of the miracle, they transfer their fear onto Jesus. They ought to have been grateful because He freed them from this dangerous delinquent, but instead they beg Him to leave. Their behavior is very similar to that of the devil, who upon recognizing Jesus begs Him not to torment him. They do not consider the liberation of the man, but the material harm that was caused by the death of the swine. It is a paradox that concerns us exorcists as well: Jesus casts out demons and is Himself cast out by men.

This is the concept of the call. In this case, Jesus shows Himself clearly, inviting in this way all those present. There is no doubt about why He did this. These people are afraid, however. How many times have we thought how happy we would be to have been in the shoes of those who met Jesus? The idea of being there next to Him leads us to suppose that under those conditions we would have had no doubts, that we could have vanquished all our fears, especially the fear of having to transform our entire life. Even though we have nothing to lose, we prefer to remain where we are without glory and without gain. It is a dramatic temptation widespread among Christians.

It is said that John Paul II was the greatest pontiff of modern times. Yet, from the beginning, he placed his pontificate under the sign of courage. When he came out on the balcony of St. Peter's right after his election, he invited the entire world to follow Christ: "Fear not, open wide the doors to Christ." It is obvious: the temptation of a utopian life, comfortable and tranquil, makes us fear Christ, who wants to place us on the path of acceptance of the cross. It is yet another paradox: we refuse Jesus because of the cross, but a life without pain, without suffering, without solitude, without death does not exist. In a word, there is no life without the cross.

What Jesus proposes is simply to accept with Him our cross, which we must in any case suffer. To accept it courageously is to transform death into life. The offer is good, even advantageous, but we still refuse it. We lack courage, we are afraid of Jesus, who wants us to be courageous in accepting and in witnessing. But this reasoning leads us paradoxically to the authentic evil of our times. Jesus is frightening. But one must ask, where are the frightening Christians today? Where is the Christian proposal that places man before the unavoidable choice of being for or against Christ? *This is the proof that we have diluted Jesus Christ. And it is precisely what Satan wants. The first weapon the world has in fighting Christianity is that of rendering it tepid, insipid, insignificant. They make it into a proposal that's not worth fighting for.*

Considering the Gospel passage from this point of view, it becomes entirely logical to compare the Gerasenes who beg Jesus to leave their territory with the devil who just before that had begged Jesus to allow him to stay in that region. *Satan desires to stay in the place where there is no room for Jesus, exactly unlike those who are touched by the love of Jesus and surrender themselves to Him would never want to be separated from Him.*

At this point, the Gospel of Mark highlights another interesting dialogue: the one between Jesus and the former demoniac, who asks to become his follower. He has seen the light and does not want to be distanced from it. *In this case too, Jesus seems to break with all messianic hypotheses that might envision Him as a warrior. He makes the man liberated from the devil understand that another type of witness is needed. All the other times Jesus heals, He counsels silence. Here He recommends testimony. And He is not afraid that it arouses a false enthusiasm for establishing a human kingdom. He is fully aware that what is testified by the casting out of demons, the true lords of this world, will not further hopes for an earthly kingdom, because it constitutes a completely spiritual battle.* The economic harm produced by the death of the swine is contrary to this logic. The Jews were forbidden to eat pork, but they were swineherds because they made great profits selling to the Romans and to the unclean pagans in general. What the former demoniac is called to witness is the liberation of man from evil: the birth of the new man, a man who can bear witness to the truth and knows how to do it well, as Mark mentions at the end of this account, because "all men marveled" who heard him.

The Epileptic Demoniac

This is a controversial episode. Many biblical scholars do not consider it an exorcism, but a simple healing. They deny, in effect, that the supposedly healed epileptic had ever been possessed. *In this narrative, however, there are many aspects that lead us to think it was a true exorcism, without even taking into account the fact that, quite often, the devil provokes certain diseases to camouflage his presence.* Another fundamental observation is that the passage highlights the way in which demons can be cast out only through the direct intercession of God, which can be obtained through faith and prayer.

In Mark 9:14–29, Jesus descends from Tabor with Peter, James, and John right after the Transfiguration. This detail is not to be overlooked. The three apostles had been dazzled by the manifestation of God's glory on the mountain, to the point of wanting to immerse themselves in it and not wanting to return. Jesus, however, immediately brings them back to earthly reality and their spiritual responsibility of bearing witness and fighting evil.

At the foot of Mt. Tabor they find many people, including scribes who are in a heated argument with Jesus' nine disciples who did not go up the mountain. When they see him, they run toward Him, and He asks them, "What are you discussing with them?" One in the crowd answers Him, "Teacher, I brought my son to you, for he has a dumb spirit; and wherever it seizes him, it dashes him down; and he foams and grinds his teeth and becomes rigid; and I asked your disciples to cast it out, and they were not able." Jesus responds with a severe reprimand, "O faithless generation, how long am I to be with you? How long am I to bear with you? Bring him to me." Placed before Jesus, the dumb spirit reacts, shaking the boy who rolls on the ground in convulsions.

At this point, Jesus asks the boy's father, "How long has he had this?" And he says "From childhood. And it has often cast him into the fire and into water, to destroy him; but if you can do anything, have pity on us and help us." Jesus replies with another reprimand that sounds like an explicit request that the father bear witness, "If you can! All things are possible to him who believes." The father gives witness in a loud voice both to his faith and his doubt, "I believe; help my unbelief!" Then Jesus, seeing the crowd rushing in, threatens the demon, saying, " 'You dumb and deaf spirit, I command you, come out of him, and never enter him again.' And after crying out and convulsing him terribly, it came out." Once the scene of healing is finished, Jesus and His disciples enter a house. They naturally cannot resist asking Him, "Why could we not cast it out?" His response is emblematic: "This kind cannot be driven out by anything but prayer and fasting."

This is a particularly complex text, in which an analysis of Jesus' question to the father of the demoniac is fundamental: it is a true indication of how to prepare correctly for an exorcism, to understand the nature of evil. We too ask the very same question, both to the person suffering the possession, as well as those closest to him, especially close relatives.

The demoniac's father explains that the boy has had this condition since his infancy. He then adds that it has thrown him many times into water and fire, indicating in this way one of the typical works of the devil: to tempt one to commit suicide, death. Another question that refutes the theory of those who hold that this is a simple epileptic is the fact that nine of the disciples of Jesus, before Jesus Himself, understand that this is the case of one possessed. They consider it a dumb spirit and they try several times to cast it out without succeeding. It makes me smile, thinking about the hieratic attitude of some exorcists convinced they can do what they do not know how to do. Other times they do succeed. Jesus Himself invited them to heal the sick and cast out demons. When they realize they are impotent and see Jesus, they understand that the solution to the problem can only come from Him.

Among exorcists, there are stories about people possessed from their childhood, even from their mothers' breast or from the very moment of their birth. These are terrible stories that always reveal the malice of man against his fellow man.

I remember one girl who had diabolical disturbances from birth. When, during the exorcism, I asked the devil what he could do against the power of Baptism received by the woman, his response was, "I got there first. Before they could baptize her, I was in her already."

A truly disturbing response, and it was necessary to understand how this could have come to pass. Questioning her parents, nothing odd emerged, no episode in the first months of life that could have aroused suspicion. Given that even in the following exorcisms the devil repeated that he had arrived first, we thought about going back in our search to the hospital where the girl was born. The mother had been admitted to a clinic in Bologna where, as we discovered, there was a satanist obstetrician who would consecrate children to the devil as soon as they were born.

If there is no human intervention, the devil is blocked. In the same way, when dealing with people united to God, full of faith, an active prayer life, a predilection for the Almighty, full of devotion for the Virgin Mary, or of special graces perhaps received through the intercession of some saint, he is also blocked. In these cases, we are protected. At the same time, there is no doubt that the prayers of the mother are valid for the child in her womb as well. So too her faith life, her drawing near to God, her devotion to the Blessed Virgin Mary, to the saints, to her guardian angel, to the blessings of priests: all are protections against the devil for the child that prays through the mother's prayer. It was once believed that the child born of a baptized woman was also baptized. The mother's consecration to God was valid for her child as well, flesh of her flesh.

In the Gospel episode, it is remarkable how Jesus asks for an open declaration of faith from the boy's father, who asked for His intervention. One moment earlier, He had boxed the disciples' ears for having failed to cast out the demon, "O faithless generation, how long am I to be with you?" Very harsh words. With the father, on the other hand, although He reprimands him, He does so with sweetness, as if his suffering were in some way a privileged status. He asks Him to have mercy "if you can do anything." Jesus' response, as always, leaves no room for vacillation: "If you can! All things are possible to him who believes." The man is given a choice and responds a bit like another famous father in the Gospel, the centurion who asked for the healing of his dying son. He entrusts himself with insistence that is both humble and convinced: "I believe; help my unbelief."

A great man of faith and a great bishop, Giovanni Battista Scalabrini, when commenting on prayer in a pastoral letter for Lent in 1905, expressed himself in these illuminating words: "Prayer is God who, invoked, descends. When it is humble, prayer not only equals but, I would almost say, surpasses the very power of God. God is omnipotent, says the prophet, and who can resist Him? Prayer, I respond."

And so Jesus, almost incapable of not welcoming the humble request of that man, hastens to grant it. *Seeing the crowd rushing toward Him, He makes haste and tries to do things without making too much show of Himself. The need to respond to the father's prayer for his son contrasts with the bothersome attitude of the crowd in search of a spectacle, incapable of comprehending the purpose for which Jesus has come. Then He addresses the spirit directly, "You, dumb and deaf spirit, I command you...."*

When the demon is cast out, the disciples are left perplexed. Entering the house where Jesus led them, desiring to withdraw from the scene, they ask him why they were not able to do the same. Jesus' answer resounds as a further confirmation that this was no simple illness, but a diabolical presence: "This kind cannot be driven out by anything but prayer."

In the Gospel of Matthew, the need for fasting is added to that of prayer. At any rate, in the Jewish world prayer and fasting were always connected when faced with a serious difficulty, an important event, or a fundamental life choice. In the episode from the Acts of the Apostles that launches Paul's journeys, the disciples of Antioch pray and fast before taking leave of Paul and Barnabas, who depart for their first voyage.

The Calming of the Tempest

For many theologians and biblical scholars, the episode of the calming of the storm is to be read as a true exorcism. I have always considered it as such. Benedict XVI articulated this thesis in a homily given in the sanctuary of San Giovanni Rotondo.

Continuing our journey through the Gospel of Mark, we find the narrative at the end of chapter four, immediately before the miracle of the Gerasene demoniac. "Jesus said to his disciples, 'Let us go across to the other side.' And leaving the crowd, they took him with them, just as he was, in the boat. And the other boats were with him. And a great storm of wind arose, and the waves beat into the boat, so that the boat was already filling. But he was in the stern, asleep on the cushion; and they woke him and said to him, 'Teacher, do you not care if we perish?' And he awoke and rebuked the wind, and said to the sea, 'Peace! Be still!' And the wind ceased, and there was a great calm. He said to them, 'Why are you afraid? Have you no faith?' And they were filled with awe, and said to one another, 'Who then is this, that even wind and sea obey him?' "

An account that we have read and heard many times, which has become proverbial, to some extent even predictable: the water, the boat, the tempest, the danger, and Jesus who performs the miracle. It seems like a painting of one of those Marian *ex-votos* that decorate and witness to the Faith in many sanctuaries. Here too, however, the obvious salvific work of Jesus is revealed in the presence of the evil one.

One must first remember that the apostles were fishermen. They knew well the dangers of Lake Tiberius, which moreover is small and not usually subject to terrible storms. They grew up on that lake and worked on it to feed their families. They would never have set sail if the weather was threatening to be violent. *But it seemed quite normal for them to take aboard Jesus to go to the other shore. The tempest broke out immediately afterward, and it was unusually violent. These expert mariners perceived it as something extraordinary. They were afraid and feared for their lives. On the contrary, Jesus slept peacefully on a pillow. The narrative deliberately juxtaposes this with the frightened disciples. His is the tranquility of one who does not fear the work of the evil one, thanks to His faith and His closeness to God.*

The juxtaposition is evident: "Do you not care if we perish? You are sleeping while all of us are about to die." Then Jesus commands the wind and the water as if they were beings animated with life itself. For good reason, the apostles and those with them in the other boats are amazed: "Who then is this, that even wind and sea obey him?"

According to the biblical scholar Emanuele Testa, it was demons that provoked the impetuous waves and winds. Their aim was to kill Jesus or simply to make Him show fear in the face of the power of evil. It was the work of the devil, who seeks our death and incites terror. In this case, he sought the death and the terror of the one who is the source of life and the origin of all that is good. Benedict XVI provides the same reading in his homily at the tomb of Padre Pio: "Jesus rebukes the wind and orders the sea to be calm, he speaks to it as if it were identified with the power of the devil." The reference is to Psalm 107, the Psalm reading in that same celebration: "For he commanded, and raised the stormy wind, which lifted up the waves of the sea. They mounted up to heaven, they went down to the depths; their courage melted away in their evil plight; they reeled and staggered like drunken men, and were at their wits' end. Then they cried to the Lord in their trouble, and he delivered them from their distress; he made the storm be still, and the waves of the sea were hushed. Then they were glad because they had quiet, and he brought them to their desired haven" (vv. 25–30).

The pope continues: "The solemn gesture of calming the stormy sea was a clear sign of Christ's lordship over negative powers and induces one to think of his divinity." For good reason, the disciples asked who it was whom the wind and the sea obey. "Their faith is not yet firm, it is being formed; it is a mingling of fear and trust; on the other hand, Jesus' confidant [*sic*] abandonment to the Father is total and pure. This is why he could sleep during the storm, completely safe in God's arms. The time would come, however, when Jesus too would feel fear and anguish, when his hour came, he was to feel the full burden of humanity's sin upon him, like a wave at high tide about to break over him. That was indeed to be a terrible tempest, not cosmic but spiritual. It was to be the final, extreme assault of evil against the Son of God."[2]

The logic here is evident. Just as he would later assault Jesus in Gethsemane, the devil whips up wind and storm in an attempt to kill Him and all His disciples. *When Jesus commanded the wind and the waters, He performs a proper exorcism. Moreover, as we have seen, the devil can take possession of objects, of animals, and of the forces of nature in his efforts to bring to completion his strategy of killing man. The devil thinks he has attained this objective when he succeeds in killing Jesus. It must be noticed in this regard that Judas kills himself too, tempted by the devil and subject to him until the very end, even when he comprehends the terrible evil he has committed.*

[2] Pope Benedict XVI, "Holy Mass in the Church of Saint Pio of Pietrelcina: Homily of His Holiness Benedict XVI," The Holy See, June 21, 2009, https://www.vatican.va/content/benedict-xvi/en/homilies/2009/documents/hf_ben-xvi_hom_20090621_san-giovanni-rotondo.html.

This is the eternal juxtaposition. God is the God of life, of the good, of goodness, of mercy, and of forgiveness. The devil is the exact opposite. Hatred, enmity, perdition, and destruction are his traits. Death came into the world through him. St. Augustine very rightly said, "if God had not given Him limits, He would kill everyone." But as we read in the First Letter of John, chapter five, "whatever is born of God overcomes the world; and this is the victory that overcomes the world, our faith." This is the raw, precise testimony of what it means to be a Christian. If one calls oneself a Christian, one must aspire to behave according to the teachings of Christ, otherwise one is not a Christian. "Let no one deceive you. He who does right is righteous, as he is righteous. He who commits sin is of the devil; for the devil has sinned from the beginning. The reason the Son of God appeared was to destroy the works of the devil. … Do not wonder, brethren, that the word hates you. We know that we have passed out of death into life, because we love the brethren. He who does not love remains in death" (1 John 3:7–8, 13–14).

During the Angelus of the first Sunday of 2010, after having reminded his listeners that Christian hope gives no value to horoscopes and forecasts of any type, Benedict XVI stated: "We trust in God who revealed completely and definitively in Jesus Christ His desire to be with human beings, to share in our history, to guide us all to His Kingdom of love and life. … The Kingdom of God certainly comes, indeed it is already present in history and thanks to Christ's coming has already conquered the negative power of the evil one. However, all men and women are responsible for welcoming Him into their own lives, day after day. … Every time the Lord wants to take a step forward with us toward the 'promised land,' he first knocks at our hearts. He awaits, so to speak, our 'yes.' "

The Second Annunciation

"Sub tuum praesidium configimus." This is the most ancient invocation of the Holy Mother of God. "Under your protection we take refuge." Entrusting ourselves to the Blessed Virgin Mary is the high road and, in some ways, the simplest path for one who wants to stay far away from the devil. One turns to Mary because one feels the need to be protected from all dangers. The history of the Church, of its saints, and of the Christian people reveals a constant devotion to Mary, which reached its high points during trials and painful situations. She has always been considered a recourse in difficult moments. For the devil, Mary is invincible. I myself have often asked him during exorcisms why he is so afraid of her, and he invariably answers, "Because she always wins, because she has never been touched by the least shadow of sin."

Paul VI said, "Everything that fights sin, fights the devil." This is the reason the devil is so afraid of Our Lady. She cannot be touched by sin. Furthermore, it is enough to read the Bible to understand this. Mary is associated from the beginning with the fight and the victory over the devil (Gen. 3:15): "I will put enmity between you and the woman, and between your seed and her seed; he shall bruise your head, and you shall bruise his heel." Mary is again presented in a struggle against Satan in chapter twelve of Revelation: "And a great portent appeared in heaven, a woman clothed with the sun, with the moon under her feet, and on her head a crown of twelve stars; and she was with child and she cried out in her pangs of birth, in anguish for delivery. And another portent appeared in heaven; behold, a great red dragon." Genesis and Revelation, the first book and the last book. The struggle that began at the dawn of time shall last until the end of time, as specified by the above-quoted passage of Gaudium et Spes*: "For a monumental struggle against the powers of darkness pervades the whole history of man ... and will continue until the last day."*

Mary is therefore associated with the work of Christ, who came into the world with the aim of destroying the kingdom of Satan and establishing the Kingdom of God. From its conception, the plan of God is Marian. As stated by Paul VI, one cannot be a Christian without being Marian. The Church does not divinize Mary, but she sheds light on her privileged relationship with the Holy Trinity, and honors her as the Trinity honored her.

It is significant that in the Bible, the Trinity appears for the first time in full clarity right at the moment in which Jesus is conceived: God the Father who sends the angel Gabriel; the Son who is incarnated in Mary; the Holy Spirit by whose work the Incarnation comes about. From that moment on, Mary is completely dedicated to Jesus, in total collaboration with Him, associated with His mission. For this reason, the rivalry between Mary and the devil is incessant and accompanies our personal struggle as well. Mary is our shield in this struggle.

The mission of Mary can be fully comprehended at the foot of the Cross. "When Jesus saw his mother, and the disciple whom he loved standing near, he said to his mother, 'Woman, behold your son!' Then he said to the disciple, 'Behold, your mother!' And from that hour the disciple took her to his own home" (John 19:26–27). Jesus entrusts us to Mary, just as the Father had entrusted Him to her. A new mission begins for Mary, a sort of second annunciation. This is a responsibility that concerns each of us, and which will last until the end of the world. Mary, Mother of the Church, is always present. The great variety of titles under which she is invoked bears witness to this. We are given the task of doing what the Apostle John did: "from that hour the disciple took her into his own home."

St. Bernard of Clairvaux claimed, "Mary is the complete reason of my hope.... We venerate Mary with all the ardor of our heart, of our affections, of our desires. This is the desire of the one who established that we should have all through her." Mary is the great gift of God. We must receive this gift into our lives. We must surrender ourselves to her, allow ourselves to be taught by her, as she taught Jesus. The work of Mary throughout the entire history of the Church is quite evident. It suffices to consider the extraordinary flourishing throughout the world of Marian sanctuaries, often the fruit of apparitions, and in each of them, their history and their witness to the renewal of faith. In the messages left by Mary in her apparitions, there always emerges the content of what can be considered Our Lady's testament, namely the last words the Gospels place on her lips, addressed to the servants at the wedding in Cana: "Do whatever he tells you" (John 2:5).

Behind every Marian sanctuary is a miraculous story tied to the rediscovery of an image, of an apparition, the vow of a people fulfilled, or that of a city or an individual. Stories of filial love around which entire communities have been built. Consider the Marian sanctuaries built on the seashore, on promontories, on hills overlooking port cities. Consider the mariners who entrusted their lives to the Virgin Mary in their sanctuaries, their voyages that could have lasted years back then. Think of their families who periodically visited those sanctuaries to entrust the lives of their loved ones to the capable arms of the Celestial Mother. In this sense, the ex-votos *of those devoted to her, who survived shipwrecks or tempests unharmed, are fascinating and can tell us, often in exquisite artistic forms, how the life, even the most commonplace, can be authentically imbued with faith and receive light and hope from the relationship with the transcendent.*

These stories and testimonies of faith distributed through time and geographical space were born and developed in very different contexts. They never propose new doctrines, only a constant reference to Jesus. Moreover, there is always an updating with the needs of the time and place in which the apparition occurs or where the miracle that led to the construction of the sanctuary is manifested. The center of these apparitions is the word of Jesus, and the worship in the sanctuaries is always centered on the eucharistic Jesus. With immense pastoral efficacy, the sanctuaries are a stimulus to conversion, to prayer, to drawing peoples closer to Jesus and to the Church. Guadalupe comes to mind, just after the discovery of America; La Salette, in such a delicate moment in the history of Europe; Banneux, in the heart of Belgium, in the midst of the world wars. And then Rue du Bac, Fátima with its extraordinary pertinence to the present moment, Lourdes with its unfathomable testimony of love. Through the Virgin Mary, the path is indicated, help is given, humanity is warned of the folly of its errors, the infinite Divine Mercy is witnessed, and man is invited to conversion and total entrustment to her. She is the universal mediatrix of graces. All grace passes through her, and she protects each one.

One must ask what would be left of the Faith of the French, or of all Europe, so heavily injured by Jacobinism, without the three extraordinary apparitions of the mid-nineteenth century: the famous Virgin of the Miraculous Medal in Paris in 1830, at the church in Rue du Bac which is still today the most frequented in Paris; the apparition of La Salette in 1846, with its prophetic message that anticipated that of Fátima; and Lourdes in 1858, with its confirmation of the dogma of the Immaculate Conception. What would be left of the Faith of the Portuguese without Fátima, of the faith of the Italians without the more than a thousand Marian sanctuaries distributed throughout the peninsula? The gospel message resounds in these places, against all heresies and the perversities of individuals and of history. John Paul II rightly called these sanctuaries "permanent antennae of the good news."

And the apparitions continue, just as the birth of new Marian sanctuaries does not stop, in every corner of the world, even the most remote. These events demonstrate that the earthly mission of Our Lady has never concluded. It continues down the centuries and in some periods is more intense, according to the needs of humanity. At any rate, neither has the earthly mission of Jesus come to an end. He Himself promised this as we read in the Gospel: "I will not leave you orphans, I will be with you even unto the end of the world."

We need only to consider the Eucharist to comprehend this. Jesus' suffering is renewed daily. In the moment in which he offered himself, he suffered in his own body all the guilt and sins down to the last man. Every time someone dies in mortal sin, part of the Blood of Christ is poured out in vain. This concept was expressed well by Padre Pio to a woman who told him about her terrible suffering, and she explained that her suffering was not that of Jesus, but certainly was more protracted over time than His, "because Jesus only suffered three hours."

The saint's response was authoritative: "You really understand nothing. Do you not know that Jesus is on the Cross until the end of the world?"

St. Paul was precise on this point: "in my flesh I complete what is lacking in Christ's afflictions" (Col. 1:24). What is lacking? Our cooperation. Our contribution is needed. "If any man would come after me, let him deny himself and take up his cross and follow me" (Matt. 16:24).

A Resource for the World

Following the line of apparitions, their messages, and their historical consequences, a true Marian pedagogy emerges, as we have said. It is as if the Virgin Mary takes us by the hand and guides us along the pathways of life, pointing out dangers and obstacles, helping us to bear our crosses. In the constant struggle against the devil, Mary never misses an occasion to help us see that she is on our side and that we need only entrust ourselves to her intercession to emerge victorious. More concretely, Our Lady points to the means we have, in our poverty, to ward off evil and to avoid it. In many messages from Medjugorje, she warns of Satan's cunning. She indicates the way of prayer and even provides the words. Nothing more, nothing less than what has happened throughout the history of salvation when the people of God, welcoming the teachings of the Lord, are able to triumph over their enemies; otherwise it is crushed. And it is by no means coincidental that in the places of the apparitions many conversions occur, many returns to the sacraments of Penance, many liberations from the devil, and many healings. The mission Christ gave to the twelve is perpetuated in Mary: to proclaim the Gospel, forgive sins, heal the sick, and cast out demons.

Every apparition, as much as it might illuminate the human condition in all its phases, is tied to its historical moment. The messages given have their particular relevance to that which is necessary for society at that moment or in the immediate future. The first great apparition recognized by the Church in our age was in Paris, in the chapel of the Daughters of Charity in Rue du Bac in July of 1830, and again in November of that same year. The visionary was a nun, Sr. Catherine Labouré. In the first apparition, Mary spoke at length with her and told her about the terrible events that were about to take place in France and Europe: "My daughter, these are sad times; terrible disasters are about to strike France, the throne will be toppled, all will be upset by calamities of every sort. (Saying this, Our Lady's appearance seemed very pained.) But come to the foot of this altar; here, grace will be given to all.... Above all, the people who ask for grace with confidence and fervor, the little and the great."

In the second apparition, she showed herself in the form of an oval medallion, and she asked Catherine to have the image minted and disseminated in millions of copies. On one side, around the Virgin Mary, from whom rays of light emanate, there are twelve stars and the prayer to obtain the graces she said she wants to disseminate among all creatures: "O Mary, conceived without sin, pray for us who have recourse to thee." This expression anticipated the dogma of the Immaculate Conception proclaimed in 1854. On the back, besides the "M" superimposed with a cross, there are the hearts of Mary and Jesus. The image was widely disseminated. Miracles began to occur soon after, beginning with the return to the Church of a schismatic bishop.

Today, the church in Rue du Bac is certainly the most frequented in Paris. The story of Catherine Laboure is also very particular, given that she was able to keep the secret of her visions from all who knew her. She spoke of the vision only to her spiritual director, who then referred the story to the bishop because she insisted on having the medallion minted. The bishop granted the request. Catherine continued to live in the same convent where all her fellow sisters wore the Miraculous Medal, although none of them were aware that the Virgin Mary had appeared to her.

The meaning of the union of the two merciful hearts of Jesus and Mary for the salvation of humanity on the back of the medal was made explicit only at Fátima in 1917. In this sense, the Virgin Mary of the Miraculous Medal can almost be considered an anticipation, or better, a preparation for Lourdes, where Mary herself said she was the Immaculate Conception, as well as Fátima.

The second great apparition occurred at La Salette, in France, a small village in the Alps of the Dauphine. It was September 19, 1846. The two visionaries, Melania Calvat and Massimo Giraud, said that they received a message and a secret during the encounter with Our Lady. The text of the secret was definitively edited by Calvat in 1879 and received the imprimatur of the bishop of Lecce, Italy, the place where she had moved. The secret announced the terrible upheavals that would sweep Europe and the world in the coming decades, from civil wars to world wars. The repeated and insistent attempts of all governments to cancel Christ from life and from the history of the nations was emphasized. Then, in the second part, which concerns us more directly because it refers to times closer to our own, the tenor becomes strongly apocalyptical, with tones that closely assume those of the vision from the book of Revelation, with the coming of the kingdom of evil and the definitive triumph of good.

In light of these visions, she invited men to pray with intensity, to do all they can so that these things might not take place. It was an invitation that was repeated in all the apparitions, and which is at the center of most of the messages of Medjugorje, where the Virgin Mary appeared for the first time ten years before the civil war in Yugoslavia, explicitly inviting the faithful to pray for peace. Concerning what must be done, Our Lady of La Salette insisted on three points, simple and comprehensible for everyone: do not swear, observe the holy Mass on days of obligation, and observe abstinence and fasting. A synthesis of Christian virtues: respect, adoration, prayer, charity, humility, and patience.

Some years after the visions at Rue du Bac, the eighteen apparitions of Lourdes took place. At a moment when atheism and rationalism were becoming the dominant ideologies, the Virgin Mary recommended penance and prayer, then made water flow as a sign of purification, of healing, and of reconciliation with God as signs of extraordinary and undying pertinence in every age. It was a strong call to a life of faith and the value of suffering. In a world imbued with positivism and egoism, the Virgin Mary made use of a poor, ignorant girl to remind people that everything depends on faith, even in the face of pain and the need for liberation. Only through reconciliation with God does one find the path, as well as the meaning of life, regardless of their circumstances. Lourdes immediately became a sanctuary of healing, recognized throughout the world as a place for the sick and the suffering. But it also became a place of conversion. Many people who might not have found physical healing there came to understand that their mission was to suffer, to bear witness that the only path that leads to Paradise passes through Calvary.

There have also been many liberations from demonic possessions or influences. *Many of the people I have exorcised were definitively liberated during a pilgrimage to Lourdes. It almost always happens in a very simple manner. They go there, perhaps after years of exorcisms, they kneel in the grotto or nearby, they pray, and then suddenly they feel liberated. For these people it is an immense joy that is impossible to describe.* There are also cases that unfold in a much less tranquil manner. Fr. Gabriele told of one elderly woman from the province of Brescia, possessed for many years, and who displayed wrathful anger whenever she saw a sacred object or heard someone praying. *After many useless attempts, her friends and relatives decided to try taking her to*

Lourdes. They signed her up for the pilgrimage with great difficulty because the organizers usually did not allow people with such afflictions to travel with groups. Before the grotto she grew restless and tried to run. Even worse was her panic when they insisted that she plunge into the pools, to the point that those accompanying her decided to force her into the water. Despite her age, her resistance was fierce, and she dragged some of them into the water with her. Her liberation, however, was immediate. None of those present would ever forget the serene face and the expressions of joy of that elderly woman as she emerged from the water.

The plan of the Marian apparitions included Fátima at the beginning of our terrible century, toward the end of the First World War. This apparition seemed to follow closely that of La Salette and announced further apparitions that followed throughout the world in decades to come. Here too, secrets were revealed. What is important is that the Virgin Mary did not so much reveal wars and catastrophes as say how to avoid them. In particular, she invited each of the faithful to consecration to the Immaculate Heart of Mary, and at the same time, asked that Russia be consecrated so that its sin would not spread throughout the world. *This latter consecration never officially took place, for the sake of not putting ecumenical dialogue at risk. And the consequences, if we wish to identify them as such, have been visible throughout the course of the century around the world, in terms of ideological contamination, the spread of atheism, wars, profanations, violence, and the suppression of entire peoples. Their perverse fruit continues to reveal itself in all fullness.*

But the consecration of the world to the Immaculate Heart of Mary did take place, based on what Jesus asked in a vision of the Portuguese blessed, Alessandrina Maria da Costa, in the 1930s. She was an extraordinary mystic who received the stigmata and who lived the last thirteen years of her life nourished only on the Eucharist. It was Pius XII who consecrated the world to the heart of Mary in

1942, in a radio broadcast addressing the Portuguese episcopate, in the presence of the Portuguese ambassador to the Holy See. The Portuguese episcopate had asked the pope to perform what Jesus had requested of Bl. Alessandrina, who at the time was still alive.

Concerning Russia, Our Lady of Fátima was proven correct. If the consecration was made and if her words were heeded, there would be peace; otherwise another war would break out worse than the present one. If the consecration was not made, Russia would spread its errors throughout the world. In the end, the Immaculate Heart would triumph. Russia would be converted. A period of peace would be granted to the world. The events have not yet occurred. *This thesis was confirmed by the subsequent apparitions to Sr. Lucia, one of the three visionaries of Fátima. In one of these, the Virgin Mary explained that since her words and her prophecies had not sufficed to convince people and since what she had explicitly asked had not been done, "God is sending me as a last resource for the world."*

Some years after Fátima, in 1933, between the two world wars and ten years before the terrible Battle of the Ardennes, at Banneux, a miserably poor and tiny town in Belgium, the last of the apparitions officially recognized by the Church in Europe took place. The visionary, Mariette Beco, was a twelve-year-old girl, the daughter of humble peasants who were not in the least devout. The conversion of her father, who was previously a committed secularist, was the sign asked by the Virgin Mary of the village priest, as a personal confirmation of the goodness of the manifestations.

Mariette was born on March 25, 1921, the feast of the Annunciation and, in that year, also Good Friday. Some days before the apparitions, she found a rosary on the ground along the road that led to the village. Mariette would point to these coincidences as signs of predilection toward her. There were eight apparitions, all during the heart of winter. The first time, Mariette was at the window. It was dark and she awaited the return of one of her little brothers. The Lady appeared in the garden in front of their home. Her face was so radiant that it illuminated the night. Mary opened her clasped hands to gesture to Mariette to come out to her, but her mother would not let her leave the house. At this same hour for several evenings, Mariette went out without saying anything and kneeled in the place where she had seen the Virgin Mary. The second apparition took place at the same hour, three days later, on January 18. Her father, who had been following his daughter's movements, saw her kneeling and busily reciting the Rosary. Our Lady appeared luminous to her, standing on a sort of gray cloud just above the ground. Mariette prayed with the rosary she had found on the ground and Our Lady prayed with her. Then she gestured to Mariette to follow her along the road leading into the village. Her father, seeing her setting off down the path in the dark of night, called to her, then went after her. Without turning around, she answered, "She is calling me." Twice she stopped, kneeled, and prayed. The third time she stopped, Mary was on the edge of a spring. She addressed Mariette, saying, "Dip your hands into the water." The girl obeyed and the rosary fell into the water. Then the Virgin Mary added, "This spring is reserved for me."

The next apparitions followed the same scheme. In them, Mary clarified in a few words the meaning of the simple message entrusted to the little girl, accompanying them with a solemn sign of the cross, as a blessing. "I am the Virgin of the poor," "this spring is for all the nations, for the sick," "I shall pray for you," "I desire a little chapel," "I come to alleviate suffering," "believe in me, I believe in you," "pray much," "my dear little girl, pray much," "I am the Mother of the Savior, Mother of God." Her last words were on March 2, when dozens of people were already gathering with her in prayer near the spring. They were simple: "Pray much."

Just a few elementary commands, in open contrast with alluring worldly desires, which are the illusions of the devil. This is the intimate, humble, poor meaning of being a Christian and a child of God: total surrender to Our Lord, recognizing in Him the wellspring of living water given to the nations, in which we find relief from our suffering, the only light capable of dispelling the darkness. From January 15, 1933, every evening in Banneux the Rosary has been recited by someone walking from the site of the apparition to the spring.

This was the Virgin Mary's explicit request once more in the apparitions of Kibeho in Rwanda: to pray the Rosary, "especially the Sorrowful Mysteries." Scores of episodes occurring between November 28, 1981, and the end of 1989 involving three visionaries, between sixteen and twenty-one years of age, all female students in a little college run by nuns, where they were learning to become teachers and secretaries. The first apparition of Our Lady was to the youngest of the three, Alphonsine Mumureke. It was November 28, 1981, just a few months after the apparitions at Medjugorje and twelve years before the horrifying massacres of the civil war between the Tutsi and the Hutu. It was lunchtime, and the girls were all in the cafeteria. Alphonsine was serving at table when she heard someone calling her: "My daughter, come here." The voice was coming from the hallway, so she went in that direction. A young woman of incomparable beauty appeared to her, dressed in white, with a veil over her head and her hands clasped. Alphonsine asked her, "Who are you?" The answer left no doubt: "I am the Mother of the Word." Then she added, "I have come to reassure you, because I have heard your prayers. I wish your classmates would have more faith, for they do not believe enough."

Altogether, the apparition lasted eight minutes. Alphonsine's classmates heard her speaking alone and did not believe her story.

They began to make fun of her and call her crazy. Over the following days she had other visions, and she prayed to the Virgin Mary to appear to her friends as well, that they might believe her. On January 12, her desire was fulfilled. The fortunate one was Nathalie Mukamazimpaka, a seventeen-year-old girl. Her testimony, however, did not help placate their skepticism. The problem was resolved on March 2, when the Virgin Mary appeared to Marie Claire Mukangango. This twenty-one-year-old woman was the leader of the skeptics. When she too told of having seen Our Lady, the entire college began to understand that something extraordinary was happening.

Something extraordinary also occurred on the morning of May 31, 2003, before the eyes of one hundred thousand people, including Cardinal Crescenzio Sepe, sent to Kibeho for the consecration of the new sanctuary dedicated to Our Lady of Sorrows. The place had become a destination for pilgrims from all over Africa, a sort of Lourdes of the continent. After a lengthy investigation, the bishop of the local diocese of Gikongoro, Monsignor Augustin Misago, and the Congregation for the Doctrine of the Faith concluded that the Virgin Mary had appeared in Kibeho. And yet, that May morning in 2003, at ten o'clock, when the solemn procession toward the new sanctuary had just begun, someone began to shout: "Look at the sun! Look at the sun!"

The cardinal, the bishop, and all present raised their eyes heavenward. The bright, hot African sun did not blind them, but allowed them to stare into it without harming their eyes in the least. Around the sun revolved a shining star, the size of the moon, in a sea of colors. The phenomenon lasted eight minutes, was seen by all present, and was documented by videos and photos. It was a sign just like the one at Fátima on October 13, 1917.

Just as at Fátima, the three visionaries had a terrible premonitory vision of blood and destruction. It was August 19, 1982. All three began to cry and tremble with fear. The apparition lasted eight hours, in the course of which they saw "a river of blood, people killing themselves, heads cut off, cadavers abandoned, flames, a terrifying monster, an abyss torn open." A vision of Hell, in other words. In that very place, twelve years later, twenty thousand people who had sought refuge inside and around the chapel that had been constructed to recall the apparitions were massacred. A slaughter that repeated itself the following year when Tutsi fired for days upon the quarter million Hutus who had sought refuge in a refugee camp at Kibeho, cutting the heads off all who tried to flee.

Another extraordinary event occurred in Kibeho. All the visionaries, despite the many apparitions, have never been able to describe the color of the Virgin's skin. She was certainly not white, but neither was she black. She was an extraordinarily beautiful woman with silky skin, to whom they could attribute neither race nor ethnicity. She herself revealed in an apparition to Marie Claire: "I come not only for Kibeho, not only for Rwanda, not only for Africa, but for the entire world. This world is on the verge of catastrophe. Meditate on the sufferings of Our Lord Jesus and on the profound suffering of His Mother. Pray the Rosary, especially the Sorrowful Mysteries, to receive the grace of repentance." She later explained to Alphonsine, "I have come to prepare the way for my Son, for your good, and you do not want to understand. There is little time left and you are distracted, distracted by the ephemeral goods of this world. I have seen many of my children lose themselves and I have come to show them the true path."

Queen of Peace

I CONSIDER MEDJUGORJE TO *be the most important of the Marian apparitions. It confronts our age with an insistence that is worthy of greater attention.* The first apparition there occurred on June 24, 1981. The six young visionaries at that time are married today and live in various corners of the world. *I immediately went to Medjugorje and met all of them. I am still in contact with some of them. They are very normal people with the same problems as everyone else. It is as if Our Lady wanted to reach the common people, families, workers, youth. Since that first period, she has been appearing to them every evening at six o'clock, wherever they might be. Every message is in line with the great pedagogical design of Mary: bring every one of her children back to her Son Jesus. She entrusted them with ten secrets which will be divulged by a priest as soon as Our Lady tells Mirjana (one of the visionaries) to do so.*

It is interesting to note that at Rue du Bac, the Virgin Mary called herself "Mary conceived without sin"; at Lourdes she stated, "I am the Immaculate Conception"; at Fátima, "I am the Virgin of the Rosary"; at Banneux, "I am the Virgin of the poor"; at Kibeho, "I am the Mother of the Word"; at Medjugorje, "I am the Queen of Peace." She is the peace of hearts that comes only from commitment to the Word, the Son of God. The miracle of the Little Virgin of Civitavecchia, on the outskirts of Rome, on the eve of this difficult moment for the Church, follows the same logic. The little statue that cried tears of blood had been bought in Medjugorje. *I knew the family for whom Our Lady cried those tears and I am convinced of the sincerity of their words, as well as the bishop's words, Msgr. Grillo, a pious and sincere man.*

As always in these cases, the confirmation of the truth and divine origin of the event comes in the form of pilgrimages, conversions, and confessions. *In Medjugorje, everyone receives what he really needs. No one ever returns home disappointed, including those who come to me for exorcisms. At the present moment, it is the one place in the whole world where the most conversions and confessions take place.*

The question remains how people can continue in their disbelief in the face of these manifestations. *Because the work of the devil in this setting is most intense. At Medjugorje, Mary herself affirmed that, every time she appeared, she was with Jesus, and then the devil always came forward. He is the one who corrupts and deceives. At any rate, there is no doubt that Medjugorje is on the front lines in the battle against the devil. It is a fierce battle, because Satan has a power he never had before: that of destroying the world with thermonuclear weapons. He knows perfectly well that he can carry out this objective, and he is working to achieve it. But he is also working hard to promote sin in the Church in his attempt to destroy it. In one of Our Lady's messages, she told how God has allowed Satan to tempt the Church for a period of approximately one hundred years, in the certainty that the devil will be defeated this time as well. Now, given that this period is about to end, Satan is more uninhibited than ever.*

Thus the difficulty, the pain of Our Lady in her constant efforts to save men and the world. Thus, her continual appeal to prayer, fasting, and conversion. *To non-believers, these practices seem useless instruments incapable of resolving even the slightest problems of humanity. But the believer knows that these means are very powerful, knows that the Rosary is stronger than all evil, than any destructive weapon. And all of us are greatly at fault here for dedicating too little time to God, despite the fact that all the time we have been given is His: an absolute gift.*

In the messages given to the visionaries of Medjugorje, the Virgin Mary has spoken quite often of the devil and his works, repeatedly inviting men to refuse him, to reject him, and not to work for him because "he wants to destroy My plans." St. Paul is firm on this matter, as he exhorts, "Do not let yourselves be conformed to the mentality of the world." This is almost like saying, "If you want to be a Christian, you must not live by adopting the fashions of the age."

The Gospel is quite clear: he who believes will be saved, he who refuses to believe will be damned. In the apparitions after His Resurrection, Jesus commands, "Preach the Gospel, cast out demons, heal the sick." We must ask ourselves if this is being done, if Christians are actually carrying out this mission. The insistence with which Our Lady appears on every continent gives us an idea not only of the infinite love of God for us, but also of the terrible religious situation our world is in, of the tremendous crisis of the clergy, of how much each of us is in need of assistance. All social classes, all professions, and the world of mass media are all disoriented and being used as instruments of corruption. *On this point, I am convinced that in the face of this massive attempt to convince humanity, there will be either a response or a chastisement. The entire Bible tells us that God is patient, patient, patient, but then comes chastisement. And we all know that it is not God that punishes; it is man who punishes himself, and men who afflict one another. It is not God who sends chastisements, it is men inspired by Satan who provoke their own chastisements.*

"Dear children. Today as never before, I invite you to pray. . . . Satan is strong and seeks to destroy not only human life, but also creation and the planet on which you live," recites the message from Medjugorje of January 25, 1991. In another message from August 1985, the Virgin Mary invites us "to enter the battle against Satan through prayer." One year later she insisted, "Only through prayer will you be victorious over the influence of Satan, wherever you are."

"Pray incessantly. Pray more. In this way Satan will be expelled from this place." Even more precise was the message of December 1988: "If you pray, Satan cannot hinder you in the least, because you are children of God and He keeps watch over you. Pray; may the rosary be always in your hands as a sign to Satan that you belong to me."

John XXIII loved to say that his day had not ended if he had not yet prayed all fifteen mysteries of the Rosary. Paul VI spoke of the Rosary as a "compendium of the entire Gospel." Leo XIII wrote twelve encyclicals on the Rosary. John Paul II dedicated important writings to the Rosary, and desired to expand this "compendium" by adding the five Luminous Mysteries with his apostolic letter *Rosarium Virginis Mariae*. He stated that "our heart can enclose in the decades of the Rosary the facts that make up the life of an individual, a family, a nation, the Church, or of all humanity. The Rosary taps the rhythm of human life." John Paul II was always explicit about his particular Marian devotion. After the assassination attempt, not only did he say he was convinced that Our Lady of Fátima saved his life, but he also immediately requested the Carmelite monks of the Church of the Transpontine in Rome for a new scapular, because his had been stained with blood. It is also well known that the image of the Virgin Mary that sustained the pope when he was shot was captured by a pilgrim present at that moment in St. Peter's Square.

When reciting the Rosary, we repeatedly ask Our Lady to pray for us, "now and at the hour of our death." Doing so, we hold perennially open the window onto eternity in the business and worries of daily life. The main characteristic of this prayer is that it is both prayer and meditation on the principal Christian mysteries. It was for this reason that at Fátima the Virgin Mary proposed the Rosary as an antidote to atheism: the man of today has more than ever the need to meditate and pray upon the great revealed truths. And we must never be afraid of being sanctimonious, repetitive, or habitual in reciting the decades. If doubt arises, just think of the fortune St. Bernadette had when she noticed that Our Lady ran the rosary beads through her fingers together with her. Just like in the apparitions at Banneux, the Virgin Mary accompanied the movements of the mouth of her little visionary while reciting the Rosary.

In fact, through praying the Rosary, we join in Our Lady's extraordinary and generous battle against the evil that appears in every corner of the world, inviting us to obey God's laws and not give in to corruption, convinced, as she herself reminds us, that the Lord created us free and that only the truth which is in Him can make us free. But in light of the Virgin Mary's insistence in asking us to pray, heeded by millions of people who meditate upon the Rosary every day and who every year make pilgrimages to the apparition sites and sanctuaries, one might doubt and ask, "Why does everything in the world seem to remain as it was before?"

I asked one of the visionaries the meaning of this incessant commitment if the world fails to convert and the moment of chastisement invariably arrives. Her answer was as elementary as it was disarming, because she too had asked Mary the same question. "The more the chastisement is delayed by your prayers, by penance, by fasting, and by works of charity, the more it can be mitigated." This was for me but another confirmation that prayer is the most powerful weapon in man's hands.

Stronger Than Evil

I visited Padre Pio for the first time in 1942 and I never stopped visiting him until 1968. I watched him as he prayed the Rosary. He called it his weapon, and his spiritual director wrote that he recited at least five every day. That must have added up to five hours a day, given the way he recited it. And the older he grew, the more he felt the need to dedicate time to prayer. His time for hearing confessions was also noticeably reduced. One of his confreres pointed out to him one day that it would have been better had he confessed for a longer period because of the many people who came from all over the world to confess to him but had to wait many days. He responded, "Do you believe the people come here for Padre Pio? The people come to hear a word from the Lord. And if I do not pray, what can I give to the people?"

He prayed a lot, but he also asked prayers for himself. He felt he was not worthy. He was terrified he might sin and lose his faith. For this reason, he was a beggar for people's prayers. I visited him for twenty-six years and I realized that it was enough to tell him, "Father, I'll pray for you," to see him radiant with joy. Then he would thank me with great enthusiasm, as if to say, "Finally, there's someone who understands me!"

I remember perfectly well how long I waited the first time seated outside his cell. When, during Confession, I told him I was a young priest, he advised me with great force, "Remember that a priest must be a propitiator. Woe to him if he is the one needing to be propitiated! Remember this well."

An exceptional man. He felt the need to sanctify himself in order to be able to sanctify others. He was also very likeable. If you had the good fortune of meeting him in a quiet moment, he told jokes in the most extraordinary manner: a true comedian. He never lost sight of his mission, though. He lived for the conversion of sinners. He was one of the few who dared to withhold absolution. It would happen in approximately a third of his confessions. But when he refused to absolve the person, you could say that he would follow that person with constant prayer. He suffered the afflictions of Christ for their conversion. He said that souls pay the price and he really did pay for them. He suffered even more acutely during the three years in which he was forbidden to confess. All the great confessors suffered intensely. The period was marked by another great confessor, Padre Leopoldo in Padua. Padre Pio would often send people to him. Padre Leopoldo absolved everyone, then did penance himself for sinners.

When Padre Pio said Mass, it seemed the bloody sacrifice of Christ was carried out once again. He seemed to be drying his sweat, but in fact they were tears he shed in his pain. He suffered before the mystical vision of the sins of humanity. He suffered participating in the redemptive work of the Savior. In the same way, the many eucharistic miracles that have happened throughout the world, like the many Marian apparitions, are another extraordinary demonstration of the love of Christ that seeks to draw us near to Him.

Jesus presses our faith. "The righteous shall live by faith," says Habakkuk. And St. Paul in the Letter to the Galatians reiterates, "The just man lives by virtue of faith." Among the great saints and mystics, it was not only Alessandrina Maria da Costa who was able to live physically and for long periods nourished only by the Eucharist. For the Curé d'Ars it had become natural to fast and meditate for hours before the Blessed Sacrament. Annalena Tonelli, the martyred lay missionary killed in Somalia in 2003, the only Christian in a heavily ideologized Islamic society, drew her strength and spiritual resources from nocturnal prayer before the Eucharist. With the local bishop's approval, she kept wrapped hidden in the poor rags in her closet a fragment left by a priest who managed to celebrate Mass every six or seven months at the hospital she ran in the Somalian inland, hiding it to keep it from being discovered and profaned.

On one side the choice for evil, and on the other, in open contradiction, the choice for good in the conviction nourished by revelation, by the insistence of the Marian apparitions, and by widespread eucharistic miracles that the Lord is urging us to have faith. He wants man to turn to him with trust because it is the only way he has to save his soul. And the Lord knows how to wait. Moreover, as anyone who looks out at the world can see, there seems to be more interest in following the devil than Jesus. We are disoriented and do not know where our true good lies. *Here we see the need to ask. For this reason, Jesus taught us the Our Father, to surrender and to ask. The Our Father is a way of keeping our pole star always before us. The Our Father is the complete gospel. And when Jesus tells us to ask the Father to liberate us from the evil one, it is because we can find the strength to assert ourselves in this battle only by receiving help from God.*

From this point of view, it is interesting to consider the prayer of Jesus on the Mount of Olives. *It is the moment in which Jesus is most human. He surrenders to the Father. He asks if it is possible to avoid so much suffering. He sees and suffers in one instant the pain of Hell suffered by millions of men. He suffers even more at the thought of how we have wasted the opportunities provided by His blood, the blood of His tears, and that which He poured out on the Cross for the salvation of men. In their mystical visions, many saints have been able to observe Christ weeping as He considers His blood poured out in vain. In Gethsemane, Jesus sought the comfort of His friends. He asked them to pray, to help Him. "My soul is very sorrowful, even to death; remain here, and watch" (Mark 14:34). "Watch and pray that you may not enter into temptation; the spirit indeed is willing, but the flesh is weak" (Mark 14:38). He felt all the weakness of His humanity. He returned and found them sleeping. Yet these are His true friends, Peter, James, and John, with whom He shared His splendor at the Transfiguration. He knew that at that moment only Judas was awake and that he was acting not on His behalf but for the devil. He experienced the loneliness of facing death and suffering, like all of us. He understood that He must accept the Father's plan if He wants to bring His mission to fulfillment.*

At that moment, the defeat of Satan was decreed. Good triumphed once and for all over evil. Now it was man, in his total and indelible freedom, who chose it. Jesus was there, always ready to welcome him. His mercy was infinite, without human comparison. "But who then can be saved?" asked the apostles, terrified by Jesus' statements on sin and on His unavoidable condemnation. His response is our hope: "Nothing is impossible for God."

This hope is nourished every day by the awareness that in this ailing society there is a great and widespread nostalgia for the good. We perceive this even when terrible things happen, when the solidarity of friends and neighbors is activated, sometimes the solidarity of the entire world. Those are moments we wish could persist under normal circumstances as well. We need a pure world, pure human relationships, good company, as we used to say. For this reason, many are overcome by desire to flee. One considers going to live far from everything and everyone. *Be careful, however, that it does not become a flight from the necessary commitment to reaffirming the good. Man was made as a social animal precisely that he might do good.*

There are also those who consider retreating into prayer, leaving behind the distractions and the crowd to dedicate themselves to the encounter with God. The aim of these people is to pray to sanctify the world, to pray to keep the action of evil far from them. With good reason, hermits since the earliest Christian centuries retreated to solitary places with the intention of praying for the salvation of the many in the cities. It is a sort of spiritual humanitarian work, which continued with the institution of monastic orders. In the light of history, we can see that it was an enormous work for the good of society and for the future of civilization, from the cultural, economic, and social points of view.

Convents and monasteries have always been situated in the immediate proximity of urban centers, in the conviction that the work of conversion and sanctification must be carried forward. The same reasoning holds for sanctuaries. Consider those that have been built where eucharistic miracles have occurred. Bolsena lies along the Via Francigena, the main pilgrim artery of Rome. The eucharistic miracle of Cebrero occurred in an isolated town in the Spanish mountains, the doorway to Galicia dominating the city of Compostela, another reference point for the great pilgrimages of Europe during the Middle Ages.

And yet evil, with all its brutality and its incomprehensible malice, is always there to question us and to instill doubts into the firmness and motives of our faith. How many times has the irrational mystery of evil put man into a corner? At that moment one can do nothing but believe, surrender to the love of Christ, and remember that one is in the school of the cross, allowing oneself to be wrapped in Mary's mantle. "If I touch even his garments, I shall be made well," thinks the woman who has been afflicted for twelve years, who, thanks to her humble gesture, is healed by Jesus in body and spirit. It is only through faith that we can return once more to the battle.

We should never be amazed at the manifestations of the evil one. Apparently, he presents himself in varied forms, when in fact he is always the same. Although it is true there are no two cases that are the same, it is also true that society changes. But the reasons for which people commit evil or suffer it are always the same. I have met people whom one cannot even get to leave their car. I took them to the church where I was performing exorcisms, but could not get them to leave their car, so great was the rage clutching them. I had to get into the car and perform the exorcism there.

In most cases, when you discover who put the curse on them as well as the reason why, you understand that everything goes back to the same logic. And on the rare occasions you meet the offender, you almost always find yourself in the face of an abyss of malice. I have also had experiences of great repentance. I remember a woman who confessed to me on her death bed that she had cursed someone. We did not know this beforehand, but she confessed it only at the point of death. There are many who have been cursed but absolutely refuse to be exorcised, just as there are many people who know they are committing evil but absolutely refuse redemption. Until the very end they reject the mercy that God offers them.

It is normal to wonder how a human being can prefer Hell to Paradise. How can one refuse the outstretched hand of God offering to lift one out of the fate of eternal damnation that awaits, especially at the moment of death, when one must surrender everything obtained on earth through evil deeds? This choice is incomprehensible only if we forget the devastating effect of the devil. But it is always a free choice; however oppressed, possessed, corrupted, or tempted man is, he remains infinitely and insurmountably free in his choice.

If one chooses the devil, one becomes capable of anything. Before the terrible massacre at Kibeho in the 1990s, the Virgin Mary warned of "a world without God, that cannot find peace because it ignores the values of the spirit." But good is stronger than evil. The course of this book has sought to clarify this. Before the devil and his works, as disturbing as they might be, the Christian has the certainty of having within (as St. Paul says) the power of the election of the sons of God through Jesus Christ. *The Christian presence in the world, accompanied by even the least witness, is a sign. By manifesting the good, souls are healed. Every man is inevitably met with the responsibility of deciding on which side he wants to be.*

The Servant of God Gina Tincani reminded her school missionaries, in words that recall those of St. Catherine of Siena: "We must take a clear and decisive stand against the error of false doctrines. The courageous affirmation of our Christian personality is a duty for us. And we have the right and the duty to give an example that attracts others." The Prophet Isaiah writes: "For Zion's sake I will not keep silent, and for Jerusalem's sake I will not rest, until her vindication goes forth as brightness, and her salvation as a burning torch. The nations shall see your vindication, and all the kings your glory" (Isa. 62:1–2).

The truth hems us in. In the face of so much hatred, it suffices to respond by bearing peace in our hearts, even just to those who are closest to us. *Never tire of invoking the help of our Lord, of asking the intercession of Mary.* She herself has come to affirm that she is at our disposal: "I am the Queen of Peace." She is the peace of the heart who simply makes a sign of wanting to entrust itself to her. The struggle is fierce, but being wrapped in the mantle of Our Lady gives us the tranquility that Jesus had on the boat in the storm. "In thee, O Lord, do I take refuge; let me never be put to shame!" (Ps. 71:1). The friend whose experience was narrated in the beginning, who was aided by Fr. Candido and Fr. Amorth to be liberated from the demonic influences of an esoteric sect, occasionally recalls (with an expression that is only apparently naïve) his simple gesture every evening: "I say my prayers and I am in the arms of the Child Jesus."

"Rejoice always, pray constantly, give thanks in all circumstances. … Do not quench the Spirit, do not despise prophesying, but test everything; hold fast to what is good, abstain from every form of evil. May the God of peace himself sanctify you wholly; and may your spirit and soul and body be kept sound and blameless at the coming of our Lord Jesus Christ. He who calls you is faithful, and he will do it" (1 Thess. 5:16–24).

Peace can be found only when one surrenders completely. This is not an easy victory, but it is something that does not disappoint, and it is something no one can ever take from you. One reaches this day by day. The greater your heart can detach itself from earthly apprehensions in order to turn to God, the more peace will invade your soul. This is a daily path of sanctity that must be resolutely willed to counter the double deceit of the devil, because sin too can enter the heart slowly. One might not even realize it, because it works patiently on our weak points. We can even mock ourselves, acting as if it were not happening, convincing ourselves that in the end, sin is not that serious. If we fail to reject it firmly, the devil systematically takes the victory. And then?

Then we start all over, with courage, with trust. We must never be afraid. In the face of sin, temptation, and the perversity of evil, the Christian must never be afraid. We have the instruments, the sacraments to fight. We must pray, indeed. We all need love. When we love, we need to be received and believed in our love. I know that God loves me, accepts me, believes me. I only need to receive Him, believe in Him. And then, I always think Jesus and the Virgin Mary are smiling at me. Are you afflicted, are you experiencing a profound distress and wanting reassurance? Place yourself before Jesus in the Eucharist and simply stay there, gazing at Him. He is smiling upon you.

It then becomes easier, more effective and decisive, even during adversity, to respond to malice and evil with a blessing. We conclude with the same words God taught Moses: "The Lord bless you and keep you: The Lord make his face to shine upon you, and be gracious to you: The Lord lift up his countenance upon you, and give you peace" (Num. 6:24–26).

Appendix

"Free Us from Evil"

General Audience, November 15, 1972[3]

What are the Church's greatest needs at the present time? Don't be surprised at our answer and don't write it off as simplistic or even superstitious: one of the Church's greatest needs is to be defended against the evil we call the Devil.

Before clarifying what we mean, we would like to invite you to open your minds to the light that faith casts on the vision of human existence, a vision which from this observation point of faith reaches out to immense distances and penetrates to unique depths. To tell the truth, the picture that we are invited to behold with an all-encompassing realism is a very beautiful one. It is the picture of creation, the work of God. He Himself admired its substantial beauty as an external reflection of His wisdom and power.

Christian vision of the universe

Then there is the interesting picture of the dramatic history of mankind, leading to the history of the Redemption and of Christ; the history of our salvation, with its stupendous treasures of revelation, prophecy and holiness, of life elevated to a supernatural level, of

3 Paul VI, "Confronting the Devil's Power," Eternal Word Television Network, accessed June 30, 2024, https://www.ewtn.com/catholicism/library/confronting-the-devils-power-8986.

eternal promises. Knowing how to look at this picture cannot help but leave us enchanted. Everything has a meaning, a purpose, an order; and everything gives us a glimpse of a Transcendent Presence, a Thought, a Life and ultimately a Love, so that the universe, both by reason of what it is and of what it is not, offers us an inspiring, joyful preparation for something even more beautiful and more perfect. The Christian vision of the universe and of life is therefore triumphantly optimistic; and this vision fully justifies our joy and gratitude for being alive, so that we sing forth our happiness in celebrating God's glory.

The mystery of evil

But is this vision complete and correct? Are the defects in the world of no account? What of the things that don't work properly in our lives? What of suffering and death, wickedness, cruelty and sin? In a word, what of evil? Don't we see how much evil there is in the world, especially moral evil, which goes against man and against God at one and the same time, although in different ways? Isn't this a sad spectacle, an unexplainable mystery? And aren't we, the lovers of the Word, the people who sing of the Good, we believers, aren't we the ones who are most sensitive and most upset by our observation and experience of evil?

We find evil in the realm of nature, where so many of its expressions seem to speak to us of some disorder. Then we find it among human beings, in the form of weakness, frailty, suffering, death and something worse: the tension between two laws: one reaching for the good, the other directed toward evil. St. Paul points out this torment in humiliating fashion to prove our need of a salvific grace, for the salvation brought by Christ, and also our great good fortune in being saved. Even before this, a pagan poet had described this conflict within the very heart of man: "I see what is better and I approve of it, but then I follow the worse."

We come face-to-face with sin which is a perversion of human freedom and the profound cause of death because it involves detachment from God, the source of life. And then sin in its turn becomes the occasion and the effect of interference in us and our work by a dark, hostile agent, the Devil. Evil is not merely an absence of something but an active force, a living, spiritual being that is perverted and that perverts others. It is a terrible reality, mysterious and frightening.

Seeking an explanation

It is a departure from the picture provided by biblical Church teaching to refuse to acknowledge the Devil's existence; to regard him as a self-sustaining principle who, unlike other creatures, does not owe his origin to God; or to explain the Devil as a pseudo-reality, a conceptual, fanciful personification of the unknown causes of our misfortunes. When the problem of evil is seen in all its complexity and in its absurdity from the point of view of our limited minds, it becomes an obsession. It poses the greatest single obstacle to our religious understanding of the universe; it is no accident that St. Augustine was bothered by this for years: "I sought the source of evil, and I found no explanation."

Thus we can see how important an awareness of evil is if we are to have a correct Christian concept of the world, life and salvation. We see this first in the unfolding of the Gospel story at the beginning of Christ's public life. Who can forget the highly significant description of the triple temptation of Christ? Or the many episodes in the Gospel where the Devil crosses the Lord's path and figures in His teaching? And how could we forget that Christ, referring three times to the Devil as his adversary, describes him as "the prince of this world"?

Other New Testament passages

The lurking shadow of this wicked presence is pointed out in many passages of the New Testament. St. Paul calls him the "god of this world," and warns us of the struggle we Christians must carry on in the dark, not only against the Devil, but against a frightening multiplicity of them. "I put on the armor of God," the Apostle tells us, "that you may be able to stand against the wiles of the devil. For our wrestling is not against flesh and blood, but against the Principalities and the Powers, against the world rulers of this darkness, against the spiritual forces of wickedness on high."

Many passages in the gospel show us that we are dealing not just with one Devil, but with many. But the principle one is Satan, which means the adversary, the enemy; and along with him are many others, all of them creatures of God, but fallen because they rebelled and were damned, a whole mysterious world, convulsed by a most unfortunate drama about which we know very little.

Man's fatal tempter

There are many things we do know, however, about this diabolical world, things that touch on our lives and on the whole history of mankind. The Devil is at the origin of mankind's first misfortune; he was the wily, fatal tempter involved in the first sin, the Original Sin. That fall of Adam gave the Devil a certain dominion over man, from which only Christ's Redemption can free us. It is a history that is still going on: let us recall the exorcisms at Baptism, and the frequent references in Sacred Scripture and in the liturgy to the aggressive and oppressive "power of darkness." The Devil is the number-one enemy, the permanent tempter.

So we know that this dark disturbing being exists and that he is still at work with his treacherous cunning; he is the hidden enemy who sows errors and misfortunes in human history. It is worth recalling the revealing Gospel parable of the good seed and the cockle, for it synthesizes and explains the lack of logic that seems to preside over our contradictory experiences: "An enemy has done this." He is "a murderer from the beginning ... and the father of lies," as Christ defines him. He undermines man's moral equilibrium with his sophistry. He is the malign, clever seducer who knows how to make his way into us through the senses, the imagination and the libido, through utopian logic, or through disordered social contacts in the give-and-take of our activities, so that he can bring about in us deviations that are all the more harmful because they seem to conform to our physical or mental makeup, or to our profound, instinctive aspirations.

Ignoring the Devil

This matter of the Devil and of the influence he can exert on individuals as well as on communities, entire societies or events is a very important chapter of Catholic doctrine which should be studied again, although it is given little attention today. Some think a sufficient compensation can be found in psychoanalytic and psychiatric studies or in spiritualistic experiences, which are unfortunately so widespread in some countries today.

People are afraid of falling back into old Manichean theories, or into frightening deviations of fancy and superstition. Nowadays they prefer to appear strong and unprejudiced to pose as positivists, while at the same time lending faith to many unfounded magical or popular superstitions or, worse still, exposing their souls, their baptized souls, visited so often by the eucharistic presence and inhabited by the Holy Spirit, to licentious sensual experiences and to harmful drugs, as well as to the ideological seductions of fashionable errors. These are cracks through which the Evil One can easily penetrate and change the human mind.

This is not to say that every sin is directly due to diabolical action; but it is true that those who do not keep watch over themselves with a certain moral rigor are exposed to the influence of the "mystery of iniquity" cited by St. Paul which raises serious questions about our salvation.

Our doctrine becomes uncertain, darkness obscured as it is by the darkness surrounding the Devil. But our curiosity, excited by the certainty of his multiple existence, has a right to raise two questions. Are there signs, and what are they, of the presence of diabolical action? And what means of defense do we have against such an insidious danger?

Presence of diabolical action

We have to be cautious about answering the first question, even though the signs of the Evil One seem to be very obvious at times. We can presume that his sinister action is at work where the denial of God becomes radical, subtle and absurd; where lies become powerful and hypocritical in the face of evident truth; where love is smothered by cold, cruel selfishness; where Christ's name is attacked with conscious, rebellious hatred, where the spirit of the Gospel is watered down and rejected, where despair is affirmed as the last word, and so forth.

But this diagnosis is too extensive and difficult for us to attempt to probe and authenticate it now. It holds a certain dramatic interest for everyone, however, and has been the subject of some famous passages in modern literature. The problem of evil remains one of the greatest and most lasting problems for the human mind, even after the victorious response given to it by Jesus Christ. "We know," writes St. John the Evangelist, "that we are of God, and the whole world is in the power of the evil one."

Defense against the Devil

It is easier to formulate an answer to the other question — what defense, what remedy should we use against the Devil's action? — even though it remains difficult to put into practice. We could say: everything that defends us from sin strengthens us by that very fact against the invisible enemy. Grace is the decisive defense. Innocence takes on the aspect of strength. Everyone recalls how often the apostolic method of teaching used the armor of a soldier as a symbol for the virtues that can make a Christian invulnerable. The Christian must be a militant; he must be vigilant and strong; and he must at times make use of special ascetical practices to escape from certain diabolical attacks. Jesus teaches us this by pointing to "prayer and fasting" as the remedy. And the Apostle suggests the main line we should follow: "Be not overcome by evil, but overcome evil with good."

With an awareness, therefore, of the opposition that individual souls, the Church and the world must face at the present time, we will try to give both meaning and effectiveness to the familiar invocation in our principal prayer: "Our Father … deliver us from evil!"

May our apostolic blessing also be a help toward achieving this.

About the Author

Fr. Gabriele Amorth, S.S.P. (1925–2016), acclaimed exorcist and Mariologist, was born in Modena, Italy, in 1925. He fought in the Italian resistance during World War II. After the war, he received a degree in jurisprudence and served as the chief assistant to Giulio Andreotti, helping him in the formation of Italy's postwar government and in the writing of its constitution. He entered the Society of St. Paul and was ordained a priest in 1954. In 1985, he was nominated as an exorcist of the Diocese of Rome, a ministry he practiced until his death. In 1990, he founded the International Association of Exorcists, of which he was president until 2000. He wrote more than thirty books, which have been translated into numerous languages.

Sophia Institute

Sophia Institute is a nonprofit institution that seeks to nurture the spiritual, moral, and cultural life of souls and to spread the gospel of Christ in conformity with the authentic teachings of the Roman Catholic Church.

Sophia Institute Press fulfills this mission by offering translations, reprints, and new publications that afford readers a rich source of the enduring wisdom of mankind.

Sophia Institute also operates the popular online resource CatholicExchange.com. *Catholic Exchange* provides world news from a Catholic perspective as well as daily devotionals and articles that will help readers to grow in holiness and live a life consistent with the teachings of the Church.

In 2013, Sophia Institute launched Sophia Institute for Teachers to renew and rebuild Catholic culture through service to Catholic education. With the goal of nurturing the spiritual, moral, and cultural life of souls, and an abiding respect for the role and work of teachers, we strive to provide materials and programs that are at once enlightening to the mind and ennobling to the heart; faithful and complete, as well as useful and practical.

Sophia Institute gratefully recognizes the Solidarity Association for preserving and encouraging the growth of our apostolate over the course of many years. Without their generous and timely support, this book would not be in your hands.

www.SophiaInstitute.com
www.CatholicExchange.com
www.SophiaTeachers.org

Sophia Institute Press is a registered trademark of Sophia Institute.
Sophia Institute is a tax-exempt institution as defined by the Internal Revenue Code, Section 501(c)(3). Tax ID 22-2548708.